Helpful Hints and Tricks
for New Moms and Dads

To Harry & Sheila & Conan! –
(Nov. 1981)

Much love
Gail & Todd

Helpful Hints and Tricks for New Moms and Dads

by Nanci Rogovin Weinfeld

Rand McNally & Company

Chicago · New York · San Francisco

Drawings by Chris Peldo

Contents

acknowledgements

To all my friends who helped me during those first years with advice and ideas on raising young children. Your suggestions were invaluable.

To my loving husband, Arthur, who encouraged me with both the raising of the kids and this book.

And, of course, the real inspiration for this book, my three children, Debra, David and Jennifer.

introduction

As a new parent you soon discover that chats with other parents eventually turn to talk about the kids.

Out of casual conversations and personal experiences came this collection of hints and ideas, to be used for your present or future needs.

May these suggestions help you further enjoy the wonderful experiences of parenthood!

feeding the family

Most new parents find the feeding of their newborn an area of uncertainty from the very first feeding baby receives in the hospital. Since all babies differ in their feeding habits you can't follow an exact formula for feeding. But baby doesn't mind if you make an occasional feeding mistake...and everyone does! The moral of the story? Relax! And give yourself time to relax by planning ahead for those harried weeks to come.

Pre-Baby

Remember that baby isn't the only one who needs to be fed. The month before arrival date is a good time to start filling up your freezer with home-cooked dinners for both of you. The foil T V dinner plates you usually throw out are perfect for freezing individual dinners of your own creation.

Or take a trip to your favorite supermarket and stock up on the huge selection of frozen dinners. You can buy everything from appetizers to desserts. In both cases, there's a plus feature: You won't have to clean plates during those tiring first weeks home.

Don't forget your canned goods—jiffy meals come out of cans as well as the freezer. And fill the shelves with snack foods for the many visitors that flock to see the newborn once you're home.

Plan ahead for hungry guests by freezing batches of brownies or favorite cookies that can be ready in no time. Plug in the coffee pot and your job as hostess is done.

To really simplify things, splurge a little and buy gay paper goods such as plates, cups and placemats so that you won't have to stand and wash dishes when other jobs await you.

Feeding Time Needs

Buy the feeding equipment you'll need before baby arrives. There's no need to wait, unless you're still debating whether to nurse or bottle-feed. Essentials are:

Bottles	A minimum of eight nursers (bottles, collars and caps) in the 8-ounce size, or three if you are going to breast-feed the baby. Two 4-ounce nursers to use for water and juice. Bottles come in either glass or plastic. Plastic nurser sets are also available, and so easy to use.
Nipples	Eight, so you'll have some spares when you need an extra in a hurry.
Measuring cup and spoon	Essential for accuracy in mixing formula.
Sterilizer	If you're using the "terminal" method of sterilizing already filled bottles. The electric model is the easiest to use. Not necessary with plastic-nurser sets.
Large cooking pot	A big soup or corn pot will suffice to sterilize unfilled nursers with the "aseptic" method. You add the formula after the bottles are sterilized.
Tongs	To lift the sterilized pieces. Maybe you already have some that you've been using for corn.
Bottle and nipple brush	A necessity for getting the bottle and nipple clean after a feeding. Get the brush with bristles at each end.
Infant seat	The small plastic ones are perfect for feeding time. Just place it on your table and baby will have a nice dining "chair."
High-chair or feeding table	Switch to one of these when baby begins to sit up. Both types work well, so buy with your budget in mind.
Feeding dish and spoon	Be sure to get an unbreakable dish.

Bibs	Four to six with plastic backings; enough for even the messiest child.
Bottle warmer	Nice, but not a necessity. Wait to see if one comes as a gift.

Formula Fixin's

If you want a little luxury when you first come home from the hospital, take advantage of the pre-mixed, bottled formula. There's nothing to do but heat the bottle and serve. The ready-to-go formula costs more but may be worth the difference if you're sans household help. You'll have no sterilizing or boiling to worry about.

Ready-mixed formula also is simple to use. Just boil the nursers and nipples for five minutes, put the filled bottles in the refrigerator and your job is done.

Liquid formula is the easiest to use when you're mixing your own. Avoid powdered mixes, if possible. They get messy in handling.

You might prefer to get the bottles ready the night before, so there will be no last-minute rushing when baby is waiting for his bottle.

And when you fill the bottles, put in only as much as you know the baby can drink. Why have to throw out unfinished portions?

Sterilizing

Remember that the lid on your sterilizer should be cool enough to touch before you lift it off. Once removed, tighten caps and refrigerate the bottles.

Try pouring a small amount of vinegar into the bottom of the sterilizer to simplify the cleaning job. And be sure to follow the manufacturer's directions for the proper cleaning method.

Bottle Time

For even heating of the formula, shake the bottle a few times while it's warming in a pan of hot water. You won't have to worry about a half-cold bottle.

9

And one more point before you begin the feeding: Your mother's trick of testing the formula on the inside of her wrist is still the best. Shake a few drops onto your wrist. If they're not too hot for you, the formula is just right for baby. If they are too hot, hold the bottle under cold tap water for a few seconds.

You can usually regulate the flow of the formula by loosening the bottle collar, if the flow is too slow, or tightening it, if the flow is too fast.

To save precious minutes at that 2 A.M. feeding, put the bottle you'll use in a filled ice-bucket before you go to sleep and keep it close at hand. When baby begins to stir, run to the closest sink and put the bottle under hot water. By the time you've changed your infant, the bottle will be warm. You'll really appreciate this trick if you live in a two-story home.

To keep your refrigerator in order, store the bottles that are ready for use in a divided soda carton. An eight-pack carton works fine.

The refrigerator should also hold any unused formula from a can or bottle, but remember to use it up within two days before germs creep in.

Do remember to rinse out all empty bottles as quickly as possible. Otherwise you'll have cottage cheese in the bottle the next day, and it's so unpleasant to clean out!

Nipples

You'll know the holes in the bottle nipples are just right if you make this simple test: Hold the bottle at the feeding angle. If the formula comes out in steady, even drops, the nipple is fine and ready for use.

If baby seems to be sucking too hard with little satisfaction, the holes may need enlarging. There are two popular ways of doing this job:

Put toothpicks in the holes and boil the nipples for three minutes.

Or, take a very hot pin and stick it into the rubber a few times.

Often the holes are too big. When this happens, there's nothing to do but throw the nipple in the garbage can and start using those extras you bought.

Gummy nipples are another matter. Before throwing them away, give them this treatment: Place them in a pan of water, add a pinch of salt and boil them for a few minutes. Now see if they are usable!

The clean, boiled nipples and caps you're saving as extras can be stored in a clean peanut butter jar. Just make sure the jar is germ-free by washing it or boiling it first.

Before you sterilize the nipples, make sure they're not clogged by filling them with tap water and squeezing the water out with your finger.

Nursing Notes

Many mothers find it a rewarding emotional experience to nurse their babies. And it certainly is an easy way to avoid the fuss of formula and bottles!

If you do choose to nurse: You'll probably be a professional by the time you come home from the hospital. While you're still there, ask the nurses and your doctor all the questions you can think of about schedules and preferred methods. This is the best time to be a "pest."

Before you begin feedings, remember to wash off your nipples for maximum cleanliness and to let them air-dry before you cover up.

For the best milk flow, it's wise to begin a feeding on the breast where you ended last time. To help you remember, pin a large diaper pin to the strap of your nursing bra on the side where you should begin at the next feeding. The trick is to remember to move the pin each time!

When you're going out for a few hours or longer, give yourself security against leaking through by putting a folded piece of plastic wrap into your nursing bra. Commercial nursing pads also work well but are made more foolproof by using the plastic wrap along with them.

Nursing moms go out too, so keep a few cans of ready-to-use formula on your shelf for those times you won't be home to nurse. Before your "mother-substitute" gives this relief bottle, however, discuss it with your pediatrician. He'll tell you what's right for your baby and what kind of formula is best.

Snoozers and Burpers

Some babies are sleepyheads and fall asleep while being fed. Try lightly tapping your baby's feet or his cheeks to keep him awake.

11

Burping is easy if you put baby in a sitting position on your lap and lean him slightly forward. Support his back and chest and gently pat him. Burping once during a feeding and again at the end will help make your infant comfortable. Not all babies burp at the desired times, but make the attempt anyway.

Water and Juice

Both bottle babies and nursing babies enjoy a drink of water occasionally. If your doctor says yes to this snack, here's how to prepare it:

Boil a pot of water, pour it into sterile bottles and tighten the caps. Or fill two small bottles with water at the time you prepare the formula and put all of the bottles into the sterilizer. Water bottles don't have to be kept in the refrigerator after they're prepared. Just put them on a kitchen shelf; they'll be ready for use in a jiffy.

When your doctor gives the "go ahead" for juice, you may find baby not as eager as you about the treat. Try diluting it with water while he's getting accustomed to the new taste.

Juice often helps to get a three-meal schedule on schedule, if not given too close to mealtime. It's especially welcome on a hot summer day.

High-Chair Hints

Once baby graduates to a high chair, he can join the rest of the family at mealtime and your feeding job will be simplified. You may eat less with baby at your side but you'll be saving time. Alternate a bite for you and a bite for baby. You'll both be finished in half the time.

For those with twins: Feed your two at the same time by propping them in a big arm chair. Use two spoons and you'll be finished in the time it would take to **feed one...or just a few seconds later!**

When your baby graduates to the high-chair but is still a bit wobbly, prevent slip-throughs by padding the high-chair further with bath towels placed around the back of the chair.

Babies are not the neatest little people, so protect your good floor or carpet with a plastic carpet runner. Slip it under the chair and let it collect the drippings.

A big piece of linoleum will do the same job. See if your local floor covering man has a leftover piece he'll part with.

To prevent the high-chair from slipping on the covering, put the legs in small round carpet protectors, the kind you put under your chairs and sofa. Rubber works best.

Bibs

Bibs come in all sizes, shapes and materials. Some are totally ineffective for keeping a child clean, so be wise and practical with your purchases.

Even before your baby is put on solids, a small bib can catch those dribbles of formula. The infant bibs come in plain or fancy styles. Baby won't know the difference, so let your budget be your guide.

As the messy stage approaches (and you'll know when!) use the large bibs that cover the entire front.

And make sure all the bibs are waterproof. Spilled food can soak right through many materials. Plastic, at least as a backing, works best for keeping outfits dry and clean.

If all the bibs are dirty, just pin a face towel around your child's neck.

Another instant bib can be made by using a cloth napkin and a spare diaper pin. This works well in restaurants.

Plates and Cups

The need for unbreakable plates and cups arises when baby begins to sit in a high-chair. No longer can you trust little hands to stay away from the food—and what the food is in.

A plastic divided dish is best. The good ones come with suction cups that help keep the dish where it's placed. (But beware—they can still be thrown over.)

This is for the self-feeders: If you have a jello mold set that came with a plastic holder about dinner plate size, let your toddler use this tray. The raised edge will keep food from going overboard.

13

When it's time for your baby to start drinking from a cup, you may meet some resistance. See if offering drinks from a plastic bottle without the nipple will ease him slowly toward a real cup.

For the cup enthusiasts! Paper cups in the 3-ounce size seem to fascinate the weaners. They fit the mouth nicely and are easily held. If you prefer, buy some small, gay, plastic cups for your child to call his own. Glass is prohibitive, as most beginners drop a cup or more a day.

When mopping up spilled drinks becomes unbearable, go to the baby store and buy a plastic cup with a weighted bottom. It should help prevent further spills, premeditated or accidental!

The weighted cup also is effective for an older child whose elbows seem to get in the cup's way at meal time.

For the unwilling drinker or milk-striker, try using a gay straw in the cup, and just see how fast the milk disappears now!

Spoons

Before your baby is six months old, your doctor will probably tell you that the time has come to start him on solids. Be sure to have your camera ready to capture the great expression that comes with the first spoon feeding!

If you received a looped-handled spoon as a baby gift, exchange it for the straight-handled type. It's much easier for both you and your baby to hold, even though the other may look cuter.

Next time you have a cocktail in a restaurant, save the long-handled plastic spoon that may come with it. It makes an excellent feeding spoon for an infant.

When baby is just getting acquainted with the spoon, put only a drop of the solid on it and put the food way back on the tongue. The food will have a better chance of staying where it should be—in the mouth.

Practice time can come between meals. Let your child play with a small spoon, but avoid the long, thin type. If baby's older sister has a tea set, maybe you can borrow a spoon. Just promise her that it will be returned!

If you misplace the baby's spoon at meal time, the tea-set spoon will be a good substitute. A small sugar spoon also will work.

The best way to help your child learn to eat all by himself is to let him use a spoon as soon as the urge hits. But supplement his efforts so that he'll get at least part of the dinner inside.

To use with the spoon: For the experimenting toddler, a butter spreader makes an excellent training knife. No sharp edges to worry about, and your child will feel so grown-up.

Clean-Up Time

A sure way of saving on cleaning bills is to wear a smock or full apron while your baby is still in that messy stage. Even if a spoonful of spinach comes your way, you're safe!

To protect yourself from baby's dirty fingers, lift him from behind when removing him from the high-chair. Carry him in this position directly to your sink and start the water.

Or bring the sink to your baby. Fill a plastic bowl with water and let your child dip his messy hands while he's still in the high-chair. Great for quick clean-ups.

A wet cloth towel also works, although it's sometimes hard to keep the just wiped hand from getting messy again. You've got to work quickly for best results.

If you decide on the "wet towel" method, have the towel ready for action by putting a hook on the back of the high-chair and placing the dampened towel on it before the meal begins. A small towel bar can also be screwed into the back of the chair.

High-chairs, too, need cleaning. For fast clean-ups, a damp cloth or sponge is the most convenient way to get that spilled food off in a hurry.

When you have the time, give the high-chair a thorough cleaning, as food has a way of getting onto the legs and back of the chair, as well as on the tray. Why not give it a thorough washing before you wash your kitchen floor each week. Food that is left on the chair too long is very hard to get off.

A very effective way to clean the chair is to hose it off outside. But stick to summer days and wear a bathing suit!

15

For variety: A gay paper placemat gives a new look to baby's high-chair tray, and also speeds the clean-up. When the meal is over, just throw the soiled placemat away.

Jars Galore

Baby food jars can fill up the kitchen shelves and become a nuisance because of their size. Be smart and make adequate room for them, as they'll be around for at least eight to ten months.

A two-tiered rubber lazy susan (they're sold in houseware departments) fits nicely on a shelf and holds a week's supply of jars. Spin it around and all the food is in view.

If you have a wooden door in the kitchen, attach small metal shelving units to the back and store the jars there. These are the kinds of shelves that are used in the bathroom closets. They're about three inches in depth, just the right size for those small glass jars.

If the manufacturer offers a free gift by sending in the baby food labels, don't wait until enough jars are empty. Take off the labels and replace them with a home-made label taped on, or use magic marker.

Before opening any jar of food, be cautious and wash off the top.

If the jar won't open for you, rap the top, face down, on a hard surface.

Save a few of the jars for storing left-overs—both baby's and yours. Those tiny jars are perfect for holding small portions of flour and sugar, too.

Ever think of using them in other rooms? Dad can keep his nails and screws in them, and they'll hold many sewing supplies, too. Fill them with those extra buttons and other supplies that always mess up the sewing basket. Everything will be in eye's view.

Preparing The Contents

An egg poacher pan is ideal for warming baby's food...especially for those who don't have that marvelous electric warm 'n serve plate. Put the different foods, out of the jars, in the individual egg pans.

Or use a divided frying pan. It will hold a whole meal and save you heating time.

The method of putting the jars in a pan with an inch of water still works. It's wise, however, to avoid this method if your baby won't be using the entire contents in one feeding. You'll have to reheat the food a second time and it may lose some of its nutritional value.

A custard dish is perfect for heating the required amount. The unused portion can stay in the jar for the next meal.

Microwave ovens are fantastic for quick heating or cooking of baby's food. Just take the desired amount from the jars, put it in a dish and heat. Make sure the food is cooled sufficiently, however.

Remember not to put the plastic nurser sets in the microwave. A manufacturer's taboo.

Always cap an open jar that will be put into the refrigerator. If you accidentally throw the cover out, a piece of foil makes a fine replacement.

For Older Children

A step stool in the kitchen makes the job of washing for meals easy and fun for your older children. And they'll be able to get their own drinks, which is a big time saver for you.

For non-apartment dwellers, a child's small picnic table placed near the back door will keep your children happy on nice warm days. Send the meal outdoors and your house will stay cleaner.

You can make custom-fitted cloths by buying the regular picnic-table size and cutting it into three or four smaller ones. The kids will love having a cloth just like mom's and dad's.

When small company is coming for lunch, bring the table indoors. At any time of the year, it will make a good "special" table. Cover it with a small paper tablecloth; it will seat four comfortably.

If your children always seem to want guests on the same day and you get too tired feeding the tribe, rotate each child's privilege to have company. You'll save arguments...in this area, at least.

better baby sitters

Discussions of baby sitters are a frequent topic at koffee klatches. Sitters come in many varieties, and their selection and hiring requires much thought and some luck. Matching sitters to families is like a blind date; it sometimes works and many times fails. Your children are your most valuable possession so take care in the selection of their sitters and you'll be rewarded.

Sitter Selection

The first evening invitation you and your spouse get after bringing your newborn home may put you into a state of panic.

For maximum security, have your folks or in-laws come over for the evening. Grandmother will be delighted to play momma again, and she'll do a fine job. After all, she's experienced.

If relatives are busy or too far away, call your pediatrician. His office may have a listing of competent baby sitters or nurses trained in newborn care. If that fails, try your obstetrician.

Or make a call to the local hospital. Student nurses usually are delighted to stay with newborns. Expect, however, to pay a higher rate for these professionals.

Are there any colleges near your home? School placement services keep listings of students who desire sitting jobs. This is a fine source for mature girls who may be willing to stay at your home for a week-end job.

Graduate students are usually hungry and are also good prospects for that week-end sitting job. If you're lucky you can often get a husband and wife team to live in. Planning a vacation? A non-working graduate's wife could possibly stay for the week.

As your baby turns toddler, the sitting routine changes. Now is a good time to try reciprocal sitting with a neighbor during the day. You'll both be richer for the exchange and so will the children.

Does the school bus stop at your corner? Wait for its arrival, be a bit aggressive and ask some of the older students if they do baby sitting. They'll be grateful to locate a new job, and you'll start building a baby sitter list.

Calling the local junior high school or high school brings good results for some. Have the placement office post cards with your sitting needs and then wait for the phone to ring.

Once you have a dependable sitter or two, ask them for a friend's name next time they can't sit. Keep this up each time you make a referred call and you'll soon have quite a long and healthy reserve list.

If you're the nervous type, try a paid trial run with that new sitter. An hour is long enough for you to make a judgement on her qualities.

Before The Sitter Comes

For a restful day or evening away from home, do a bit of before-leaving homework.

Prepare a list of emergency numbers and post it near the phone. Include the number of your destination, your closest at-home neighbor, doctor, hospital, police and fire department.

A permanent list of important numbers can be taped to the underside of table phones in all rooms. This will be helpful for you, too.

It's easiest for child and sitter if you do the preliminaries such as pajama selection and bed preparation, especially with a new sitter.

If you'll be gone through the dinner hour, bring out the T.V. dinners. They're tasty and so easy to prepare. Don't forget to instruct the sitter on oven use, however.

Once The Sitter Arrives

To avoid misunderstandings later, set the rules before you leave about visitors, food and phone use. Don't wait until trouble brews.

Also take the sitter on a tour of the house. Point out phone locations, entrances, bathrooms and the children's rooms. Searching for a ringing phone can be a frustrating experience in an unfamiliar home.

Make sure your sitter knows the location of diapers and fresh clothing in case of spills. Time spent hunting for these through closets and drawers is time away from the care of your child.

If a storm is threatening, make sure that a flashlight and candles are accessible. Black-outs can be frightening in a strange home, and dangerous.

When callers or deliveries are expected, tell the sitter who is coming. Otherwise, opening the door to a stranger should be taboo.

Time to leave and baby needs changing? Let the sitter do the job. But if she's a bit nervous with the crying baby, tell her to do the diapering on the floor or on a big bed. It will lessen her fear of your squirmer.

For Reluctant Children

Your favorite sitter will often fail to please your toddler. Want some advice?

Give the sitter some small surprise or candy to give the upset child before you leave. That usually wins friendship quickly.

Engaging a sitter and child in a cooperative task works wonders. Save dessert time for when you leave, and let your child and the sitter make an ice-cream cone or drink together.

Never sneak out the door without saying good-bye. And always explain to your youngest, in understandable terms, where you're going and when you'll return.

If all else fails, remember that the pitiful crying will most likely stop within minutes after you leave. So enjoy yourself and your evening out without feeling guilty.

If bedtime comes before you leave, inform the kids that a sitter will be coming. Be honest, because not having mommy and daddy home can be disturbing if they wake up.

For The Working Parent

With so many working parents, satisfactory day-care arrangements for your child are a must. Care should be taken in deciding the best option available, ranging from a sitter in your home to an infant-toddler center or regular day-care center.

If you prefer to have your child remain at home, advertising in the local newspaper will most likely bring the best response from prospective sitters. You can also send bulletins or make calls to senior-citizen centers and your local churches.

Allowing yourself two weeks or longer for your search for a parent-substitute will give you time to interview, train and become acquainted with your new sitter.

When the phone starts ringing in response to your ad, it helps to have a list of questions handy to help you do a preliminary search. The following is the questionnaire that I used and found very effective:

Name?	Married?	Single?
Address?	Phone?	
Age range?		
Children at home?	Ages?	
Own car?		
Experience as sitter?		
Other job experience?		
Hours available?		
Recent references?		
Come for interview?		
Able to do other chores?		
Expected salary?		

If you can get someone to help with household chores, so much the better. How nice it is to come home to a straightened-up home. Be prepared to pay more for this luxury, however.

If possible, invite your final choice to spend a day with you before you go off to work. It will make leaving much easier on that hectic first day back to work.

A marvelous form of day-care is often in your own neighborhood. Taking your child to a neighbor who watches small children can be a plus for you and your child.

Pre-arrange a short visit at the sitter's home for you and your child. Leaving should go smoothly from the start.

Don't forget to talk about food needs, diapers, naps, clothing changes, rules on illness, payment and other concerns.

Infant-toddler centers are springing up now that so many parents work. Be sure to visit all those in your area so you can compare facilities, staff and program before making your important, final decision. A second, unplanned visit will give you more confidence in your choice.

clothing clues

Buying infant's clothing seems to be an area of delight for most new mothers, and a disaster area for husbands and the budget. Months before baby is due you will probably go to your favorite children's store looking for the perfect layette, and from that day on, the selection and care of clothing will be part of the fun of being a parent. However, buying clothes and getting the maximum wear from your purchases also is a challenging job that only you can handle, so see how clothes-wise you can be.

To Buy Or Not To Buy

Store layette lists are often padded with extras that you won't need, so try to be cautious when you do your buying. You can always fill in with those extras later.

Below is a list of clothing basics that should fill the needs of your baby for the first six months.

Diapers   Four dozen seem to be a good amount to buy if you will not be using a diaper service. With this amount, you'll be washing two or three times a week.

Under-   Four to six cotton shirts with or without sleeves, depending on
shirts   the season.

Rubber   Buy four to six pairs. Without them, you'll be washing sheets and
pants   clothing daily.

Sleeping Four to six is a good number.
gowns

Kimonos or Sacques	Remember, styles will vary with the season.
Sleep 'n play outfits	These are the greatest! Have at least three. They come in different fabrics and styles and will keep your baby ready for any occasion.
Sweaters	Two are enough. One for wear and the other for the washing machine. Orlon is preferred because it doesn't irritate delicate skin and is easy to care for.
Cap	One cap for those cool winds.
Booties	One pair. Ask for the T.V. booties that tie at the ankle. They really stay on.
Bibs	They get so dirty fast, so buy at least six. Plastic backing will keep outfits drier.

To protect baby, wash any of the layette items you bought that were not in sealed packages. Dirty hands may have handled the items before you.

If you want a strictly pink or blue layette, remember that you can pick your layette before the baby is born and then phone in your color choice after the arrival.

If twins are a possibility, why not purchase your layette from a store that will give you another one free if a double arrives.

A Word About Sizes

The temptation to buy too many infant outfits is common to all. Babies change so quickly that the three month size is too impractical and is outgrown in no time, so see if you can hold yourself back from buying more than the baby really needs.

Start with the six month size for sleepers, crawlers, and underwear, even though your baby will look lost in them at first.

And don't hesitate to return some of those outfits that came as gifts for more practical clothing in the larger sizes. Your baby will have a nice wardrobe waiting when the little outfits are outgrown.

And Now About Sales

Stock up on your tiny tot's needs at the National Baby Week sales that are held in March. It's a good time to fill in with the extras you waited to buy. The January white sales will help you in the towel and sheet department.

Want to save 30 to 50 percent on the price of a snowsuit? You can if you wait until the winter clearance sales are held, usually in January. Buy one for the following year if you're pretty sure of the size your child will need.

You can save even more by shopping at local resale shops or at garage sales. Money saved can really add up.

Pre-season sales are smart investments, too. Although the savings are less, you can usually save around 10 percent if you want to be an early-bird.

Being Practical With Time And Money

A one-piece bunting is a good purchase as it is so much easier to put your small baby into than an infant's snowsuit. You won't have to struggle with squirmy little arms and legs. Just zip, and off you go!

You'll find that the overalls with the fasteners in the crotch are a good invest-ment, too. Diaper changes go so much more quickly when you don't have to pull down the whole overall.

And speaking of time and energy, you'll save plenty of both if you are practical and buy wash and wear clothes. They really do come out ready to wear. Just be sure to keep those special washing instruction tags that come with the clothes. You can hang a little cork bulletin board in your laundry area and pin the tags on that.

Want to save money? Buy your first child gripper pajamas in colors that can be worn by a younger sister or brother. Check motifs and designs carefully, as lit-tle boys don't like hearts and flowers.

While your children are still pre-schoolers you can get away with buying them slacks, sweaters and shirts that may be worn by either a son or a daughter.

A basic style winter coat, such as a camelhair, that has buttons on both sides also will look fine on a boy or girl. You can easily dress it up for your daughter by sewing a small fur collar on the neckline.

Try not to be a hand-me-down snob. Young children seem to enjoy wearing their cousin's clothes for a change, and what could be more welcome than an extra snowsuit or play outfit for that already tight budget.

Diapers, Diapers, Diapers

You'll probably be handling diapers for two years or longer. Make life easier for yourself with some shortcuts.

With the aid of a modern washing machine, you no longer have to pre-soak diapers in special solutions and containers before washday. Just set your machine on the pre-soak cycle and your job is done.

With an older machine, improvise by stopping the machine after the proper water level is reached. Just lift the top and let the diapers soak for 10 minutes or so. Then put the top down and re-start the machine. And don't forget that hot water is the best.

If you prefer to keep diapers in one piece, use only the recommended amount of bleach when you wash them. Check the instructions on the bottle carefully, as over-bleaching will cause breaks and holes in the fibers. Using more than the required amount won't get the diapers cleaner, anyhow.

Diaper pails need to be washed, too! Wash them easily in your big laundry tub at the same time you're using the machine. Put the pail under the rubber hose during the rinse cycle and the suds from the rinse water will clean the pail out. But better stick around to hold the pail during this procedure.

Incidentally, a tall, plastic trash container with a swinging top or removable cover makes an excellent diaper pail substitute. It will look pretty, too.

If you're using a deodorant cake inside the pail, check to make sure it is safe from curious fingers and mouths. Tape it to the inside of the pail with strong adhesive tape, if you're not sure.

And spare yourself those expensive plumber's fees! After rinsing a diaper in the toilet, be sure to remove it immediately and put it in the pail. If you don't someone is sure to come and accidentally flush it away. The result can be costly.

Weekly laundry service for baby's layette is offered by most diaper service companies. It is a wise investment for your first weeks with a newborn, even if you have your own machine. But keep in mind that if you are to enjoy this service, you'll probably need a greater number of the essential items of clothing.

If you are going to treat yourself or be treated to diaper service, it's a good idea to check out the various companies for prices and service. There may be slight differences among companies in your area. It's a good idea to keep a spare dozen diapers on your shelf for emergencies.

If you don't use a laundry or diaper service, you'll find that using disposable diapers during baby's first few weeks at home will help you regain energy before the real chore of washing diapers sets in.

Disposables have lots of uses besides the traditional one. Try putting one under baby when a change is needed or use them as lap protectors. They make good shoulder protectors at baby's burping time. The large size placed over the crib sheet will give added protection from spitters.

Also, keep an extra box of disposables in baby's room for those frequent lazy days when you don't get to the washing machine in time with the filled-up diaper pail.

Cloth diapers have their uses, too. For a quick clean-up job, wet a clean diaper with warm water and clean baby's bottom in one motion. It's easier than using those small cotton balls or wads of wet toilet paper. Just check your diaper supply to make sure there's enough left for baby.

Pre-folded diapers make the diaper ritual easier for you. They're ready to put on without additional work on your part.

If you remove the pre-folds from your dryer and pile them up before they are 100 percent dry, they'll be smooth and soft when needed.

Now about those diaper pins: When old pins refuse to go into the diapers, rub them in your hair for a few seconds and they'll be oiled instantly. A breeze!

You may also store the pins in a small cake of soap and get the same results. Take the pins out of the soap and you'll find they slide in with ease. (And you'll know where to find them at changing time.)

By the way, baby will like it if you cover the top of his changing table with a receiving blanket. He'll love the warm, snug feeling, especially in the winter.

Shoes, Old And New

Do your children have their new shoes looking old in about two weeks? With a little effort you can restore their lost beauty.

If you keep a small box of crayons in your shoe-shine kit, you'll have a ready supply of instant shoe colors to fill in small scuff marks on those worn shoes. This is especially helpful for the one pair of purple shoes your daughter insisted on buying.

Do her party shoes look played in? You can make patent leather shoes shine again by cleaning them with petroleum jelly. Spread it on with a cloth and then wipe off. It will help prevent the patent from cracking, too.

If the patent leather on her black party shoes is worn off in spots, a black felt-tipped marker can be used to fill in the little scrapes.

Most sneakers and canvas playshoes may be machine washed. They should not, however, be put in the dryer because the heat will melt the rubber. Let them air dry instead.

If you want a quick clean-up for the rubber on dirty sneakers, apply rubbing alcohol and rub hard. You'll see those dirt marks disappear!

But why not keep the dirt where it belongs? Outside. Place a brick outside the entrance door for scraping excess mud and dirt off the shoes. The kids will think it's fun and your floor will stay cleaner.

Let your vacuum cleaner work for you, too. Clean boots on the inside by using the hose of your vacuum, without the attachments. The dirt will be gone in seconds.

For shoes that come home wet, stuff crumbled paper or toweling into the front part of the shoes and the shape will be retained. (And next time encourage boot wearing.)

After a trip to the shoe store, rub the leather soles of children's new shoes with an emery board to make them skid-proof.

Two short strips of adhesive tape, attached to the soles of new shoes, will also work. Remove the adhesive after the first or second wearing.

Here's another trick that's effective. Scrape new soles on a rough surface such as a sidewalk or a brick. Accidental falls due to slippery soles should now be eliminated from your household.

Shoelaces seem to have a habit of ripping just when your children are going out. If you keep a supply of laces in assorted lengths and colors to replace the ripped laces, there will be no frantic moments spent looking for a mate.

As for the daughter who insists on wearing her party shoes to school daily, why not let her wear the party shoes for two days and the school shoes for three, if that's agreeable to both of you. (Warning: Girls being what they are, this hint can't be guaranteed foolproof.)

Rain And Snow

Winter-time depression is an ailment common to all young parents. Anyone with pre-schoolers around has probably had the symptoms. Some possible remedies:

For loss-proof mittens, take a long piece of heavy yarn and attach it to the top of both mittens. Put the mittens through the coat sleeves with the yarn going along the inside of the back of the coat. The mittens can't escape.

If you have no yarn handy you can cut two pieces of sewing elastic, three inches long. Sew one end of each piece to the top of the mitten, and put a safety pin in the other end. Now pin the mittens to your child's cuffs. They'll stay there until you want them off.

Still, it's best to buy two matching pairs of mittens for each child. You'll avoid that frantic searching for a misplaced one and also have an extra pair on hand for those days spent out in the wet snow.

If it's an in and out day, rush to your dryer with the wet snow outfits as soon as your child comes inside the house. In a few minutes the clothing will be ready to be worn again.

And be a helpful parent by buying pull-on or snap-top boots. Little hands find zippers very hard to work.

One way you can help with coat zippers is to tie a small piece of strong cord through the zipper pull. It gives the child something to hold while his hands are still so small.

29

You can replace that pulled-out drawstring in a jacket hood by attaching a big safety pin to one end of the cord and working it through the hood with your finger. Better not forget to knot both ends of the string so you'll avoid a repeat of this whole thing.

This works well! Small, plastic bags put on over children's shoes will make boots go on with ease. The bags will also keep shoes and socks drier.

And now one your child's teacher will be grateful for. Label all boots, sweaters and mittens with your child's name or an identifying symbol. It always happens that there are 10 other red boots in the same class, and they all look alike.

Getting Dressed

No experience seems to frustrate moms and dads more with little children than dressing time. When the urge to scream sets in, it's time to try new methods.

Is there a high-chair or stroller handy? Put your baby or toddler into it if he makes a fuss when his shoes and socks need to be put on. This will give you control over his kicks and wiggles so that you can complete the dressing job.

A favorite trick for three and four-year-olds who just can't seem to get their coats on right is to put the open coat on the floor and have your child sit down into the coat and put his arms into the sleeves. He can now stand up and finish the job of getting dressed. Simple?

Allow plenty of dressing time in the morning for children who go to school. It can take from five to twenty-five minutes for a nursery-school-age child to get himself dressed, and pushing never works.

See if your child is willing to pick his outfit the night before. Dressing time will then go more quickly in the morning--provided he doesn't change his mind about his last night's choice!

Let your kids really enjoy the playground or park by dressing them in sturdy play clothes. Your child will relax more knowing that you won't get angry if the outfit comes home filthy.

And why not let your daughter wear her best dresses when she wants, even though it's not party day. Wouldn't you rather have a well-worn dress with a spot than a new dress that was outgrown and put away?

Washday Wonders

Washday woes have you down? No one really enjoys washday, but there are some ways to give the old chore a new twist.

Put a gaily colored, plastic trash container in each child's room. It makes a great hamper and can be left in a closet or inside the room. When washday comes around, just go from room to room collecting your load.

Wear Them Longer

With a stitch or a snip, you can add months of wearing time to your children's clothing and stretch the budget, too.

You can have an instant nightgown for your toddler if you just cut off the bottom edge of a sleeping bag that's become too short. Hem the cut edge and admire the finished product.

The feet on gripper pajamas always seem to rip before the rest of the pajama. Just cut off the fabric at the ankle and hem the new edge. It is better than throwing the still-good bottoms out.

An edging of wide rickrack, fancy trim or ribbon sewed to the hem of a favorite dress will prolong its wearing time. Cover the hem mark and give it a new and different look.

And here's an easy way to stretch the wearing time of coveralls and jumpers that have buttonholes on the shoulder straps. Just move the buttons down to the edge of the strap and you'll gain as much as an inch in length.

Another dollar saver: If your daughter arrived before your son, take her pink snowsuit to a professional dry-cleaner and have it dyed navy or dark green. It's cheaper than buying another outfit.

New Uses For The Old

Do you feel guilty about throwing out or packing away clothing that could somehow be used again? If you're not sure just what to do with it, try some of these ideas:

Let your old maternity tops protect you from your little spitter. They are very handy as smocks when you're carrying your baby. Also keep one handy for visiting grandmas who want to stay clean and formula-free.

Baby can have a smock, too! A kimono can double as a smock for your baby. If it is put on with the snaps in the back, it will keep his outfit clean and dry until show-off time.

Do you have a collection of unused or faded terry-cloth hand towels? They make cute bibs when you cut a neck hole and bind them with bias tape. Try decorating them with appliques for an added touch.

You can keep blouse sleeves and shirts clean at feeding time, too, by making protective cuffs for them. Use the ribbed top of an adult's old sock and reinforce it with elastic if necessary. These protectors are easy to wash and may be used over again.

Your daughter will like this. An old receiving blanket makes an ideal doll cover for her doll buggy and cradle. It will also keep her favorite doll warm and snug at feeding time.

And why not save those worn baby clothes and old plastic pants for her doll's wardrobe. The small and medium sizes should be just perfect for her larger dolls.

For The Next One

Another of the fun parts of parenthood is the packing away of the outgrown clothing in anticipation of the arrival of another baby.

After your first has outgrown his clothing, wash everything that will get put into storage. Stains and spots are so hard to remove if they have been allowed to set over a long period of time.

But don't waste your time ironing outgrown clothing that is to be stored away. Wrinkles set into the clothing while they are waiting to be worn and you'll have to do the chore all over again.

Mark the sizes on the inside labels of clothing with a marking pen. You'll have an easier time sorting clothes for your next one if you take a few seconds to do this now.

Save any big television boxes or clothes cartons that come your way. Store that outgrown clothing in them and be sure to label the boxes as to size, season and sex.

And have a special box for layette items that either boys or girls could wear.

Closet Tips

With a little luck, a little discipline and a few simple store-bought aids, you can keep your kids' closets looking fairly decent.

Hang an expandable wooden hat rack in a back closet for your children's hats, coats and mittens. They can hang the clothes up by themselves if the rack is hung at a low level.

Let your children take and put away their own clothes by placing an extension rod at their level in their room closets. This can be very effective, if the kids cooperate.

Is your closet floor covered with dirt? Plastic boot trays, left in your closet all year long, will help keep the floor free from the inevitable dirt from boots and play-shoes. The trays are easier to rinse off than the floor. Vacuuming will rid the trays of pebbles and mud, too.

You'll eliminate last-minute searches for a matching pair of boots if you use clip type clothespins to hold a pair together.

And More

There's really no need for those drawstrings that often come in the top and bottom of your infant's clothing. Take them out. They may choke the baby if pulled accidentally.

Falling shoulder straps can annoy even a crawler. The problem can be solved by crossing the straps in the back and putting a safety pin on the inside of the fabric where the straps meet.

Buttons on children's clothes seem to pop off so often. If you use heavy thread for sewing the buttons on coveralls, jackets and coats your mending chores will be made lighter. It's also a good idea to reinforce buttons on new coats before the first wearing.

It's so easy to ruin the decorations on fancy dresses. Turn the dress inside out before ironing fancy ribbon or lace trims. The heat of the iron can ruin the decoration very quickly when direct contact is made.

For the leather look: Shorten dresses of vinyl or leather by turning the hem under and gluing it to the inside of the fabric.

If your little girl has fine hair, look for barrettes that have rubber on the fastener. The rubber will help keep her hair neat-looking and in place.

Try colored pipe cleaners for pigtails, ponytails and top-knots. You can cut them in half for your very young daughter. You'll hear less screaming because they won't pull or snag the hair.

easy eating

Cereal

Cereal is usually the first solid baby will eat. Most parents go with delight to the food store to purchase a box of baby cereal immediately after getting the go-ahead from the doctor. Baby is now on the road to "eating."

Baby cereal is traditionally mixed with milk or formula. Your baby will want time to get used to that first solid, so give the cereal fairly "milked down." Try stirring the cereal into the milk rather than adding the formula or milk to the cereal. In a few days you can make it thicker and in correct proportion.

If you have the green light for juices, start by adding a teaspoon or two of juice to the oatmeal to give it a new taste plus added nutrition.

Older children somehow make the switch from hot to cold cereal with very little coaxing. With the multitude of cold cereals on the shelves, it's no wonder every child finds some brand to his liking. For variety, a ripe banana or other fruit gives a new taste. If your child insists on adding sugar to the already sweetened cereals, do the job of "sugaring" yourself.

When baby is sitting with the older children, take a handful of their cold cereal and put it on the high chair tray. Baby will love munching on the bits while you prepare the "baby breakfast."

On Weekends Only

Keep cold cereals on a shelf within reach of the children so they can help themselves to breakfast. Pour milk into a plastic pitcher the night before. Great plan for those 6:00 A.M. risers.

Put some graham crackers, that have been left upstairs, into baby's crib to keep him pacified for a few extra minutes until you get out of bed.

The cereal-egg breakfast, sold in the baby food section, is ideal for lazy Sunday mornings. Heat right in the jar and serve. Your job is done.

Eggs

Egg yolks are another recommended first for baby. They can be prepared in various ways, so experiment until you find your favorite method.

The easiest, but most expensive, is to purchase the already cooked yolks in the baby food department. This is fine for an occasional treat for the cook.

But you can hard-boil three or four eggs at once and put the yolks in a clean baby food jar. Use the needed amount at each serving and store the rest in the refrigerator.

Another alternative: Put the yolk only in a custard dish, place the dish in a pan of boiling water and wait for the yolk to cook. Easy!

If baby dislikes the taste, mix the egg yolks into his cereal.

The whole-egg eater has more variety to choose from. Eggs can be hard-boiled, soft-boiled, scrambled and poached.

If soft-boiled is the favorite, try crumbling a piece of buttered toast and mixing it in with the egg.

Or spread a poached egg on a piece of buttered bread, cut it into quarters and breakfast is ready to be eaten.

Lunches

Lunch time offers a considerable variety, especially for the young baby. Prepared baby foods come in an ever-increasing assortment of meals.

Once baby graduates to table foods, usually with the arrival of a few teeth, your choice of foods widens even more.

A good place to shop is at the "home-cooked" foods section at your supermarket. Ask the clerk for one or two pieces each of cooked ham, roast beef, turkey roast, and other sandwich meats to make baby's menu well-rounded. Most clerks won't mind the small quantity if they know whom the meat is for.

Many cold salads are tasty. Try a few out by buying ¼ pound each of such things as chicken salad, ham salad, jello salad and other permissibles. You'll see which baby prefers without much waste.

Cheeses, too, are tasty and nutritious. No need to serve only your favorites to your baby or toddler if you buy just a piece or two of a few different types for him.

For the sandwich eaters: Vary the shapes of the sandwiches and watch them disappear. A cookie-cutter is just the answer for a bit of variety and fun.

Ever try dipping a sandwich, such as ham and cheese, into a beaten egg and then frying it for a few minutes? It may spark the appetite.

For lunch box carriers: When it's hard-boiled egg day, why not take a magic marker and draw a funny face on the shell? Kids love surprises, especially when they're at school.

Ever think of writing a personal note on your child's lunchbox napkin? It's especially nice coming from the working parent!

Soups And Meats

After you stop at the home-cooked food section, go directly to the fresh meat department and begin your shopping for baby's meat dishes.

For just-right-portions, buy a pound of ground meat. When you get home, divide the package into little patties, wrap them in foil, label them and put baby's own meats into the freezer. Now there's no need to worry about "what's for dinner" where the baby is concerned.

Want to cut the family's roast up so baby can eat it, too? The fastest way is to roll a piece jelly-roll style and then slice it.

Leaving enough meat on the bone for your toddler is smart. Children seem to eat the meat more readily and with ease if it's on a bone rather than cut up. Chicken, steak and chops are perfect.

Still having trouble with an un-eager eater? See if baby fruit mixed into chopped meat increases the appetite. Or mix a simple cheese sauce, such as American cheese mixed with milk, into the meat.

Speaking of soup: If your child is a non-soup eater, put his soup in a cup. The speedier process of drinking soup may increase his desire.

Vegetables

Vegetables seem to have the lowest rating on the preferred food list. If you're clever, you can up its position in your house.

One of the first rules is to be careful not to grimace when feeding the vegetable you dislike most to baby. He'll catch on to your childhood dislikes in a short time. Spinach really isn't so bad!

You can take devious measures to get good results. Ever put honey on disliked vegetables? It helps sweeten the taste.

Instead of buying baby jars of vegetables, try mashing regular cooked vegetables or putting them into the blender for a minute. The end result is very close to the quality of the baby food.

Vegetables added to jello in small quantities may be enticing. Mince them fine and add to thickened jello. Try carrots and celery for starters.

If cottage cheese is a favorite, add a teaspoon of a grated raw vegetable the next time you serve it. Proceed slowly, however.

Another trick is to mix the vegetable into chopped meat and give it all in one swallow. This is especially good for peas.

Vegetables au gratin add new taste to ordinary fare. Just sprinkle some grated cheese or bread crumbs and butter on the vegetables, brown for a few minutes and then serve.

Throwing out that extra ear of corn? Don't! Put it in the refrigerator until needed for toddler's meal. Slice off the corn, heat and serve. Use other leftovers for baby, too.

Potatoes

Potatoes can be served in many ways. One of the easiest to prepare for baby is the no-fuss instant mashed variety. Follow the directions on the box. They're ready to eat in five minutes.

Incidentally, mashed potatoes are a fine spoon-training food, as they won't fall off the spoon readily.

Molding mashed potatoes into various shapes is a novel idea that promotes good eating. Give your creative hand a try.

Having potato pancakes for dinner? Make a few miniature ones for your toddler, too, but fry them in butter rather than oil to make them more appealing.

Fruits

If vegetables are still a non-preferred food, substitute fruit. Fruits are nutritious and tasty and seem to have greater appeal.

Don't forget to wash fruits before serving them to remove any spray or dirt that might be on the skin.

Ripe fruits are best for a young child as they're less likely to cause stomach upsets.

Ripe fruit added to cold milk is a welcome treat. But be sure to put the combination in the blender before drinking to get the right consistency and color.

Many fruits can be sauteed, sugared or baked. Experiment with your favorites and see what appeals the most.

Milk

Milk, one of the daily essentials, causes many parent-child arguments. If your child doesn't like milk, you can serve milk substitutes and not feel guilty. Cheese and puddings made with milk are both excellent substitutes. Check with your pediatrician about your own child's milk needs. See what he advises.

There are some tricks that you can try, if you must. Adding a drop of food coloring may be an effective aid. Who can resist pink milk! Or add a teaspoon of chocolate syrup for delicious drinking.

Bring out the blender and make your own milkshakes. Serve in a gay cup and watch the milk disappear.

For a sick child, a milkshake with an egg blended in makes a nourishing meal, especially for a child temporarily off solids.

And for emergencies: Keep a box of instant milk on your kitchen shelf. You never know when the dairy may call a strike.

Juices

Baby juices, found in the baby food department, are recommended for your juice drinker. They come in so many flavors, baby is sure to like a few.

Heating juice is not advisable, as it loses some of the vitamin value. Room temperature is fine.

When he graduates from baby juice, you can try making your own fruit juice in the blender. But remember to strain it before serving.

Ever think of serving unthickened jello as a drink? It's nourishing and adds variety to the menu for a once-in-awhile treat. Good cup-training drink, too.

Ice cubes tinted with food coloring are fun for young children and help entice their appetites. Put some in the next juice glass.

Desserts

How nice it would be if all the courses were consumed with as much gusto as desserts usually are.

Even baby food companies score when it comes to desserts. You can save pennies by buying their junior-size desserts instead of the baby-size jars. Some fruits and desserts are almost identical in texture but cheaper in the larger jar. Check for yourself.

When your child graduates to puddings and applesauce and can eat raisins, use a few to decorate these favorites. Make smiling faces on the surface.

For the toddler who likes to bake: Buy the small cake and muffin mix packages. They're an easy and fast dessert treat.

Rolled, uncooked cookie dough is another quickie. Your little cook will love helping you prepare these.

Cakes and cupcakes can be even more appealing when decorated with colored shot. Cutting cake into unusual shapes also adds variety to a regular dessert.

To prevent frosting from getting all over your child's fingers and clothes, cut the frosted top off and replace it inverted. This also solves the problem of frosting sticking to waxed paper in lunch boxes.

For ice-cream lovers: Fill a safety cup ice-cream cone just to the top and flatten it. You'll have less spills.

Popsicles also make desirable desserts. They can be homemade and are more nourishing if made with fruit juice. Orange juice freezes well.

To prevent dripping, push the popsicle stick or ice-cream bar through a small paper plate before serving. Plastic cup covers work well, too.

Snacks

Snacks and desserts are interchangeable, although the eating of snacks is usually not encouraged by most parents. But since all kids like to snack, make the limits known to prevent arguments.

Remember: Nuts, popcorn and hard candies are strictly forbidden for very young children. They can choke on those foods too easily. Save those treats for the older children, only!

Instead of making candy a forbidden food, try leaving some around in a dish. Your child's craving for candy may be reduced when it is no longer a forbidden luxury. Or allow one piece after every meal.

Many children are content to snack on fruits and vegetables. If you encourage this type of snack, you may be one of the lucky ones.

Teething Foods

Teething babies enjoy munching on something tasty. Most stores have a good selection of biscuits and pretzels that won't crumble. They do seem to satisfy the biting urge, so try a box or two.

Zweiback is an old favorite. Save money and make your own by cutting up 2-3 day-old bread into ½" strips. Place them in a shallow pan and bake slowly (225° F.) until browned, turning them occasionally.

Zweiback also is effective as a pre-meal pacifier. Next time baby cries and must wait a few minutes for his bottle or meal, give him a piece of zweiback. Bagels, too, are excellent for teething babies.

A Few Extras

When introducing new foods, try one at a time. If an allergic reaction sets in, you'll know what the culprit is. Your doctor will appreciate this, too.

When it is new-food time, feed the baby the new food just at the start of the meal when he's hungriest.

Even the youngest will appreciate appetizing meals. Avoid monotony by having a variety of colors and textures on the plate.

And last, think of yourself when you try to force your child to eat. Could you stand having someone constantly telling you how much and what to eat? You set your own limits--and baby does, too.

bathtime brighteners

Bathtime receives a high score on the baby chore scale. It is often the favorite time of day for parents, especially if baby responds favorably to the water. Make it an unhurried time in your home, and both baby and you should enjoy the relaxed pace. A smart mom or dad will have all the bath items assembled before splashdown begins.

Bath Articles

Here's what you need:

Bathing tub	Anything from a bathinette to a small dishpan will do.
Wash cloths	Three or four tiny ones.
Towels	Baby towels are available, but you may prefer using your regular terry towels.
Cotton balls	For cleaning ears and eyes.
Baby oil, lotion and powder	Not necessity items, although they feel good to baby.
Baby shampoo	Your favorite brand.
Comb and brush	A soft brush, sold in an infant set.

Tubs 'N Baths

The big bathtub should be reserved for a future date. Newborns are hard to handle in a large tub. The kitchen sink is a great solution and you'll save your back, too.

If a sponge bath is on the schedule, wash one part of the baby at a time, starting with the face. Wash and dry each area before going on. Save the diaper region for last.

Have the O.K. for the first tub bath? No need to fill the tub with more than 1" of water.

And to make sure the water is not too hot, use the reliable "elbow" test. If the water feels right to your elbow, it will be comfortable for baby, somewhere between 90-100 degrees.

Did you know that the warmth of the water will have a relaxing effect on your newborn? Plan your feeding schedule accordingly or you may have a very sleepy baby to contend with.

Bathtime over? Wrap baby up in a big beach towel for a cuddly feeling. The winter baby may appreciate having a warmed towel, especially on those cold, cold days.

And have the layette items ready. Keeping them near the bathing area will save steps and time, and dressing time will go more smoothly.

Before putting on the fresh diapers and clothing put a dab of power on that nice clean body. But don't over apply. Powder can have an irritating effect on the lungs if inhaled.

Bathinette Graduates

Now that baby is in the family bathtub, your job is simplified. However, the wee bather still may need steadying, so have him sit on a towel that has been placed on the tub floor. For further slip-proofing, add some safety strips. They come in all shapes and colors to add a gay note to the decor.

In a hurry? For the fastest wash job, try a big sponge instead of a face cloth. Baby should be clean with just one soaping and one thorough rinse.

44

Tub toys will make baby's bath a special treat. Bring in the summer beach toys, wash off the sand and add them to the water, along with the "rubber duckie."

Have an old terry towel around the house? Make it into a simple hand-puppet and watch it perform. It can be used as an extra wash cloth, too.

While your older toddler is having his bath and water fun, use the time to straighten out the linen closet in the bathroom or clean out the medicine chest. See how much you can accomplish?

Do you want some variety at bathtime? Try a stand-up shower-bath. The kids love it and it's so fast and effective. Just put the bath faucet on and you have an instant shower.

Hairwash Time

Some children seem to love the weekly hairwash routine. And then there are some who find it an unavoidable but hated ordeal. Want to know how to make this a pleasant time for all kids?

Buying a no-sting shampoo is the safest way to avoid tears. Read the label to your child to gain his trust. Now he'll know you aren't teasing.

Tub hairwashes seem to be the favorite among young children. Just be sure to have a sponge or face cloth handy when the drips start running down the face.

One way to avoid the drip-in-the-face is to have your child lean backwards under the tub faucet. This is a quick and easy method. Do it before you run the water to avoid getting soapy shampoo water mixed with the clean bath water.

If the above suggestions still bring on tears, invest in a pair of swim goggles, the small size. Next time it's hairwash hour slip the goggles on your child's eyes and watch the smiles.

Practice Makes Perfect

Bathtime also can make swimming an all-year-round activity for your toddler. The tub is a perfect practice area for breathing exercises, dunking of the face and other swimming skills. Next summer he'll really be in shape!

Haircuts

With the price of haircuts soaring, why not perfect your own style of cutting for both your boy and girl? It's cheaper and much quicker than making a trip to the barber or beauty shop.

On a warm day, do the job outdoors. You'll spare yourself the task of cleaning up the fine hair from your floor.

Before you begin, bring out the high-chair or youth chair to save your back from aches and pains. Your child will sit more comfortably, too.

Now cover your child's shoulders with an old towel or plastic smock to eliminate a case of the itches. Even a long strip of paper toweling secured with a safety pin will do.

Inside or out, clean-up will be a speedy process if you spread newspaper under the barber chair. An old plastic tablecloth will do the trick also.

Does your daughter scream and squirm when you approach with the scissors? Put scotch tape on her bangs and cut below the bottom edge for a straight look. Try this with your son, too.

If all else fails, resort to bribery. A candy bar is cheaper than the price of a professional stylist. But only use this when you are desperate and that hair is getting unruly.

bedtime beckons

One of the first items on your baby list will be to purchase a crib and dresser. Equipping baby's room can be quite challenging. In most department stores the juvenile furniture section is jammed with the latest "his" and "her" matching bedroom sets. Styles in natural woods and heavenly blues and yellow to make you wish you were a baby again. It's hard to resist the elegant sets, but remember, babies aren't fussy and won't object to your choice be it plain or fancy.

Equipping The Bedroom

Here's what to buy:

Crib	Old or new, fancy or simple.
Bumper pads	Baby will appreciate these.
Waterproof mattress	Spend your money here and buy the best you can afford.
Mattress pad	To protect your investment.
Sheets	Try for three fitted sheets.
Crib blankets	Different weights according to the season.
Chest of drawers	Keep future needs in mind with this purchase.
Lamp	A blessing for the 2 A.M. feedings.

Bassinettes

Bassinettes are still in style, but their use is limited to the first two or three months. If grandma insists, take her antique with a smile.

Cribs

When the offer of a free crib comes your way, be grateful. Wonders have been performed on used cribs since the coming of antique-finish kits. Refinish that old chest of drawers to match and wait for the compliments. Caution: Make sure the paint is child-safe.

Gay appliques cost pennies and give zest to the old wood-stained crib. Ever think of covering the end sections with bright contact paper? It's so easy to put on.

Cribs come in various sizes, the six-year size being the most popular choice. But if you're cramped for space in a small apartment, settle for a portable crib or a four-year size. Remember, the size doesn't necessarily correspond to baby's age.

Speaking of cribs, it's best to switch your number one child from crib to bed a month or so before baby's arrival. This will prepare your toddler for the take-over of his former property and help ease the feelings of jealousy that often result.

Did the furniture store forget to come on the specified date and you're home from the hospital? Pull out a big drawer, pad it with a pillow and presto- instant crib. Then get on the phone and call that store! A playpen also makes an excellent crib substitute, for naps or longer periods of sleep.

Sheets and Mattresses

Tired of changing sheets? A large unfolded diaper placed along the top of the crib should help. When baby spits up, you can change the diaper, not the sheet.

Or try this. Put the soiled end at the foot of the crib until washday arrives. Just don't tell your immaculate friends who may find this unsatisfactory.

Don't forget to place the mattress in "low" position for your second born. He'll be protected from anxious siblings who hover over the crib trying to wake him up or take him from the crib.

For longer use, switch the mattress position periodically so that wear and tear will be evenly distributed. This is wise for other household mattresses too.

Naptime

Naptime—what a marvelous invention! If you're tired, too, now's the time to take that well-deserved rest. Or catch up on your routine chores.

"Baby Resting-Please Don't Disturb." Make two signs and hang them on the front and back doors so that the two of you can have a pleasant, uninterrupted nap. This works wonders the first few weeks at home when the gift man keeps arriving.

Do you live in a two-story home? A baby carriage makes a perfect bed for a nap indoors. If you bring the carriage into the living room or family room, there will be no need to run the stairs for sleep-checks.

If your baby won't sleep? Take a short ride in the car and see what the results are. A walk around the block in the carriage may also induce sleep.

Did you know that receiving blankets can be used to promote sleep in a restless baby? Wrap your newborn snuggly and see the calming effect it has. Nothing like a security blanket!

And Bedtime

Your hard day is almost over when bedtime approaches. Hopefully, baby will be agreeable and leave you with a few hours to do your own thing.

If not, save an ounce or two in the evening bottle as a reserve tranquilizer. When a sleep resister balks, the milk will soothe him. This works best in a quiet, darkened room.

Once sleep finally comes, put a toy or two in the crib for morning fun. You may get some extra sleep in the morning with this arrangement. But wait until his eyes are shut. Toys left in the crib before baby goes to sleep may stimulate his playing instinct.

Mobiles are fascinating to the "up" baby. Ever think of making your own? Just check the original creation for safety features.

Sickness Strikes

Many unexpected days will be spent indoors when childhood illness arrives at your door. Colds and other ills can't be avoided, so do your best to ease the pain.

One of the most effective, leak-proof ways to administer medicine to a newborn is to use a medicine dropper slipped into the corner of the mouth. Propping baby slightly will help the medicine go where it should and help prevent choking, too.

For bottle babies, putting liquid medicine in the nipple is an effective trick. Caution: Don't do this too often, as baby may begin to refuse his milk out of protest.

Giving medicine to the sick, squirming toddler can be quite a chore. Put him in his high chair, hold his hands tight and pop the medicine in. You may need an additional helper with this.

A vitamin dropper is the solution when the two-year-old balks at spoon medicine. Less spills and tears.

A spoon full of sugar may be the solution to horrible tasting medicine. Have the sweetened spoon ready to go into the mouth as soon as the medicine is swallowed.

Remember that all medicines should be out-of-bounds for your explorers. Even aspirin, when taken in quantity, can be fatal, so play it safe and keep medicines out of reach.

Fooling your child into taking medicine also is a mistake. Medicine is not candy, even though it may come in cherry or orange candy-like tablets. Don't encourage your child to take more than he should by using this ploy.

Temperature up and you don't know what to give for it? Gather your medicines from previous illnesses and bring them to the phone with you when you call the doctor. It may save you time and money for a new prescription.

Always throw away any medicines that are marked with an expiration date. They can be dangerous. It's good to make a periodic medicine chest check for discards, and to have your pharmacist always include an expiration date on the label.

Children in Bed

No one likes being confined to bed, but an ingenious you can make it a more pleasant experience.

Using bright paper cups and plates will add some cheer to sick-in-bed meals. And think of the germs that won't be spread when you use these throw-aways.

Keep the foil plates from TV dinners and fill them with surprise dinners of small portions. When served in the foil on a bright and sturdy tray, they're bound to make the appetite increase.

When boredom sets in, bring out the "sick box." In a plastic or cardboard shoe box put little beads, crayons, scissors and other scraps for youthful creations.

A new box of crayons and activity book also will help pass the day. Maybe you can draw along, too. Sick children sometimes need the extra attention.

To avoid clutter, set up that spare snack table or bridge table next to the patient's bed. At least everything will be off the bed and in one easy-to-reach spot.

To Cure the Ills

Minor ills pop up without much notice, so be prepared.

Keep a dishpan in storage and when stomach flu strikes, put it next to the bed. An old wastebasket will do the same job.

Want to save more clean-up time? A towel tucked into the side of the bed will give the bedding and mattress extra protection at flu time and also spare the child embarrassment.

Cut lips respond well to an ice-cold wash cloth. Sucking on the cloth is easier than struggling with ice cubes.

And speaking of ice cubes, for quick and painless splinter removal, put an ice cube on the splintered area for a few seconds, first.

Emergency Strikes

Too often panic sets in at emergency time. By learning the ABC's of first aid you should gain some confidence.

First aid courses are offered at nominal fees in most adult education programs. Check with your local school office for schedules of classes.

In a real panic situation, call the fire or police station. They'll arrive in minutes and will drive you and your injured child to the hospital. Don't attempt it yourself if your child needs your immediate attention, or you feel too upset to drive.

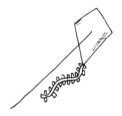

playtime pleasures

Play is the chief occupation of young children and watching them play alone or with others can be a delightful adventure. Providing your children with the proper setting and the right equipment for meaningful play is an important job that is challenging, but also fun.

Buying Toys

Before buying any toy, be sure that your child is ready for it. Often the age level printed on the box is not right for your child. You be the judge of its suitability.

Rummage sales can be great fun for both you and your child. Many bargains have been snatched up by the wise shopper. Puzzles, records and other toys are usually plentiful and can be purchased for a fraction of the original cost.

A word of caution: When purchasing a toy at a sale or in a store, always check to see if all the pieces are there so that you won't have a disappointed child when it's time to play.

It's wise to clean off the new purchases when you get home, as they may have been collecting dust and germs on the shelf.

Avoid buying fancy china tea sets and glass toys for your pre-schoolers. Plastic toys are much safer and more practical. Warn grandma about this one!

Stuffed Animals

Stuffed animals are a delight for children of all ages. Buying well-made animals is a wise investment.

Before your baby gets his new cuddly teddy bear, check for loose eyes or other parts that could be pulled off by little hands and swallowed.

Ever try cleaning a dirty bunny rabbit with dry cornstarch? Rub it into the fur for a few minutes and then brush it out. The animal will look freshly bathed.

For a more thorough job: Many stuffed animals can be machine washed using the gentle cycle, but check the labels first. When you remove them, brush them out a bit.

Air dry any animals or dolls with plastic trim. The plastic might melt in a hot dryer.

The Toy Box

Once there's a baby in the house, there's also clutter, so one big, sturdy toy box is a necessity. If you are buying one, invest in a well-made one because you'll probably be using it for many years.

Making your own? A big flat coat box makes a fine storage bin for toys and can be tucked under a crib or bed. Decorate it with paint or contact paper.

Need another? Cover a carton with something pretty and use it as a spare in the living room area. It's especially handy in a two-story house. When company comes, hide it in the closet.

For a spare, try a gay-colored plastic laundry basket and keep it where the clutter concentrates. When company comes, quickly pick up the toys and toss them in the basket.

Your picking-up chores will be lessened if you provide shelves out of your toddler's reach for your older child's precious games.

Every three or four months make a toy box check. Take out any outgrown or broken toys and give them away or throw them out. But be sure to do your toy "weeding" job when your kids are asleep or away. They seem to delight in keeping every toy that is theirs, regardless of condition. And make sure discards go in the outside garbage cans. Indoor wastebaskets don't do the out-of-sight trick.

Playpens

Playpens serve a useful function for both you and your child. They keep the baby out of harm and mischief and save you the time and worry of constantly watching his movements.

The mesh type pen is a wiser buy than the pen with wooden slats because your baby won't bump his head when he is learning to stand.

A playpen is a great refuge for a newborn. Put the baby in an infant seat and place the whole bundle inside the pen. He's now safe from the older children who are playing nearby.

Or try reversing this process. Put your three-year-old in the pen for privacy when your crawler begins to get into the games that aren't meant for him.

If your child gets fussy in the playpen, try moving it to a different spot. Add a new toy or two and you could see a smile again.

If that doesn't work, try amusing your cranky child by putting a soothing record on the phonograph. He may delight in moving his body to the music. It's good for his intellect, too.

Putting the playpen near a low window or near the glass patio doors will give a new perspective to your baby's world. Even a moving leaf can be exciting. Help your toddler see the outside world, too, by placing a small child's chair or stool near a front window.

And speaking of the outdoors, an old playpen in the backyard makes an excellent, safe play yard for the under one-year-old.

A big porch, if you're so lucky, also makes a perfect spot for a playpen. Your baby is safe and still in view of what's happening on the lawn.

Instant Toys

Toys come in all shapes, sizes and prices. With a little imagination you can provide unique toys without stepping into the local toy store.

Do you have any colored, non-scratchy scouring balls hidden under your sink? They're just the right size for little hands to play with. No chance of breaking your favorite vase, either, if your pitcher begins to practice.

Is there a bird in the house? Borrow his mirror with the attached bell that is hanging in the cage. It's just the right size for a little baby to play "peek-a-boo" with, and the jingle will add extra delight. Be sure to scrub it off, however, before baby gets it.

Wash off some of your extra plastic hair rollers and watch your little ones have fun rolling and chasing them, or nesting them inside each other, if you have assorted sizes.

A nest of boxes can be made inexpensively by just saving assorted gift boxes in different sizes and covering and painting them, if you want to brighten them. Children love to play with boxes, so why not use what you already have.

For the block lovers, it's easy to make a set of blocks out of plastic milk cartons. Take two halves and tape them together, then cover them with contact paper.

Your older child can use the containers to make houses and buildings. Don't forget to rinse the containers before using them, however, or the toy will be useless the next day.

When you don't have time to be so constructive, give your toddler some old newspaper or wrapping tissue to rip up. Just make sure it isn't daddy's evening newspaper that's being ripped.

Balloons are a favorite toy, so keep some handy for un-special occasions, too. Inflate them just enough so that they can be caught and not so large that they'll pop.

This is for grandpa's house: Take out the poker chips for your toddler. Throwing the chips around and then fitting them back in the poker chip case is amusing and challenging. It's a bit hard at cleanup time but worth the effort. This is a great time waster when boredom sets in.

For Three's, 4's and 5's

Save a few baby food jars and let your child's imagination do the rest. Pencil holders and banks are simple to make with this just-the-right-size jar.

When there's nothing to play with, bring out your button basket and some string. Unusual bracelets and necklaces can be made from your one-of-a-kind assortment.

There's no need to buy lacing cards when they're so easy to make. Either draw an original or paste a simple one-object picture on cardboard. Get out the paper punch and a long shoelace and your child will be ready to begin.

Puzzles also can be homemade. Take a bright picture from a magazine, paste it on cardboard and get out the scissors. Now cut the picture into assorted pieces (the size of the pieces depends on the age). Presto————a new game!

Next time you're left with an extra big carton, think twice before throwing it out. Just cut off the ends and your kids will have their own tunnel.

If you are really imaginative, use such a carton to create a doll house for your daughter. Cut out the windows and doors and add some trim. Add a bit of paint and you'll earn yourself the Best Parent of the Year award.

Is your child in need of a secret hideaway? Bring up the old card table and cover it with a blanket. Remember————no adults allowed.

This is a favorite: Stuff a sock and put it over an old broomstick to make a unique horse. With some buttons added for eyes, mouth and nose, your cowboy is ready to go.

The same broomstick can become a balancing board, although a rather narrow one. If it's kept on the floor, hard spills can't occur.

And when it snows: An old pot and a long-handled wooden baking spoon are perfect for scooping up all that white stuff. You can always do your cooking later.

Water Fun, Indoors

A kitchen sink filled with water and liquid dishwashing soap seems to draw children. Try filling your sink with this mixture and throw in some plastic bowls for added fun. Don't forget to have your child stand on a waterproof, slip-proof chair, however.

Warning————suggest this activity before floorwashing time if you want to save your nerves. Things get messy when water is around.

Here's another sink game. Fill the sink with the above ingredients and this time add a few drops of food coloring. Take out a hand beater and let your child beat the water. He'll see colored bubbles appear.

57

If you're busy in the sink area, a large dishpan filled with water makes a fine sink substitute. Float a small, plastic boat in the pan for your child's amusement, and add a few drops of blue food coloring to the pan. Your child will now have a blue sea of his very own.

There's no need to keep spending money on store-bought soap bubbles. Buy just one jar and when it's empty, fill it with homemade bubble stuff made of liquid soap and water. Make sure the wand is not thrown out. But if it does disappear, don't fret. Take a drinking straw and improvise. Make four small slits in the end and bend back the edges. It should work.

Now that the bubbles are made, be smart—and safe—and send the kids outdoors. Bubbles travel and can land on your good furniture.

Water Fun, Outdoors

Even an infant can have fun in water. Put him inside a rubber dishpan and let him float inside a wading pool that has only a few inches of water in it. Don't leave him alone, however, for even a second.

When buying that wading pool, be sure that it can be emptied by one adult, you. Most large plastic pools are too heavy to lift after they're filled with water.

If no hose is available, fill the pool using your biggest soup pot. The pool will be filled in no time. Two or three potfuls are enough for a small pool or a small child.

Lukewarm water from the kitchen sink is often preferred to the cold water that comes from the outside faucet. Check your child's preference first.

To get the child out of an icy pool, add one pot of hot sink water. This is faster than waiting for the sun to do the job; the kids can plunge right in.

For the diaper set: When the wading pool becomes community property, it's wise to add 1/8 or 1/4 cup of chlorine bleach to the water. Just don't encourage drinking water from the pool.

For a real treat, put your child's favorite bubble bath into the wading pool when you're filling it up. This is a sure child pleaser...and the kids will get clean, besides.

Here's another sneaky tactic: when the pool is forsaken as a swimming spot, the kids may have fun using the water to wash the outside patio or sidewalk. Just bring out a pail and a sponge.

58

Remember that your neighbor's child may be delighted with the sight of a filled pool on a hot day, so when it's time for your family to go indoors, empty the pool out first. A filled pool can lead to tragedy.

What about a pool that won't stay filled? Before giving it to the garbage man, try mending the leaks with rubber tire patches and rubber cement.

For real economy, there's that old favorite, the turned-on lawn sprinkler. Lower the water spray for the toddlers. And think of the benefit to your grass!

More Outdoor Fun

Playing in the sand is a toddler's delight. Instead of having your garden destroyed, supply a safe spot for sand play. Protect your child, too, by covering him with a shirt if he'll be in the hot sun for awhile, or cover him with some good protective lotion.

You can buy a ready-made sandbox in a department or toy store, but for less money you can provide a homemade fun spot for your children.

Sand is sold in bags at lumber stores and garden shops. The salesman can tell you the correct amount for the shape and size of your box. Or take a trip to the beach if you want "authentic" sand. Bring those big, plastic trash bags and fill them up.

Now dad, go to the tire store and buy a big, used tire for a sandbox unique. A truck tire is great. Fill the center hole with the sand and throw in a few pails and shovels. The kids can sit on the edge of the tire and begin their sandcastles.

A plastic wading pool that is no longer used for swimming also makes a fine sandbox. If you don't have an old pool, convert a small, new plastic one into a sandbox. They're often cheaper than the custom boxes.

If dad's handy, he can buy some wood and nails and delight your youngsters with the result. A sandbox is not difficult to construct. Paint it a bright color, fill it up and it's ready for use. While dad has the tool case out, have him put casters on the bottom so that you can roll the box in or out of the sun.

Now some work for mom. Homemade pillows will make nice seats for the children and keep them a little cleaner. Use washable materials so that they can be thrown in the washing machine at night and be ready for the next day's play.

Keep the cat out! It's a good idea to cover the sandbox at night with a plastic sheet or a piece of oilcloth. Secure the covering with four bricks so that the animals will have to go elsewhere.

Sand sticks. It's a hard job to get sand off of your child after his play in the sandbox. Taking the sandy clothes off at the back door, if you can, is smart. It's better than letting it get tracked onto your floors and furniture.

For the child that refuses to undress, at least insist that his shoes and socks come off outdoors.

Swing Away

Bring the park to your backyard by adding a real favorite————a swing set. This is sure to bring years of use (and abuse) by kids of all ages, so it's smart to buy the best your budget allows.

Swing sets come with various equipment from seats for your infant to climbing towers for your eldest. The important consideration is durability. Be careful in this department.

Remember, it takes two to put up a swing set, so get a helpful friend or relative to give you an assist. You'll need it.

Once the set is assembled, be sure it's secure in the ground. You can buy safety units to keep the legs of the set in place. If you're certain you won't be moving, why not cement the legs in. That always works.

All children need to be reminded of the swing set rules, such as not running into a swing, using the slide correctly, etc. Your under-two really needs watching and protecting. Standing behind your little one during his first attempts on the slide steps will give him confidence in no time.

Covering the wooden seats that may be on your set will make any accidents that do occur a bit less painful. Try covering them with rubber car mats tacked underneath.

Some neighbors pool their financial resources and buy their play equipment together. Each neighbor buys a different piece of equipment and the kids rotate backyards. It works!

More Equipment

Send dad to the junk yard for an old steering wheel. Attach it to a big block of wood and your kids can "drive."

For coordination skill: A balance board is simple to make. At the lumber store get a board about six feet long and five inches wide. Put cinder blocks under each end and it's ready to use. A coat of paint will give it a nice, smooth finish.

If you're lucky enough to get your hands on an old pickle barrel or similar barrel, your children will have a fine tunnel with little effort on your part. Just cut or saw the ends off. The pickle barrel may need a good scrubbing and airing first.

When It Rains

Open the garage door and let the older children roller skate around their new rink, the garage floor. This is advisable only when the floor is clean and minus the family car!

The cement floor in your basement works fine, too. And the little one can ride his tricycle down there in safety.

When "there's nothing to do" rings out in your household, surprise the kids by giving them that "something to do." A rainy day box filled with colored paper, paste, scissors and crayons is bound to amuse a restless child.

A new supply of coloring books and punch-out books that you've kept well-hidden will delight your little girls. A new truck or puzzle should work for your son.

Ever try giving the children a new dime store scrapbook and some paste? Save your old magazines and catalogs and see what original picture books evolve.

This may work, too. Let your restless one pick a prize out of a special surprise bag. Have some inexpensive toys and games gaily wrapped and ready for the next bad weather day. Grandmas———take note. This is fine for your house, too, for those unexpected visits by little people. They'll think you're so thoughtful.

You know those little trinkets and toys that cereal makers delight in adding to the box? A cereal prize bag will solve that "who gets it?" problem when there is more than one child in the house. Collect the toys and toss them into the bag. Alternate turns in picking a prize.

Playing With Others

Playing with the neighbors usually starts when your infant turns toddler. It's a fine idea to invite other toddlers to your home for some socializing.

For the very young, an hour is long enough for at-home entertaining. The older pre-schoolers can go longer, if play is going smoothly!

If your first child is fortunate to have young cousins around, let them play together often. Relatives can tolerate more aggression between their children than can two new mothers with tiny children.

For your older children who leave home base: Instead of screaming their names at dinner hour, how about using an identifiable whistle or bell to call the kids? It's much more effective than shouting and more pleasant to the neighbors' ears.

If your child is a long distance traveler, attach an old alarm to his bike and set it at the desired return time. This should do the trick and save you many phone calls at dinner time.

The type of key chain that has a meter reminder on it makes a fine alarm clock substitute and can be attached to the bike. You'll have to shop around for this item, but it works well.

safety suggestions

Safety is one area in which all the responsibility falls on you. An infant or toddler does not have the ability to sense danger in the seemingly safe environment of his own home. Where safety is concerned, second chances may not come so plan ahead and make sure you've baby-proofed each of your rooms.

In The Bedroom

If you are going to use second-hand furniture in baby's room, check all the labels on the paint you'll be using to give new life to the crib and dresser. It should be baby-proof paint and will say so on the label. Some babies teethe on their pretty furniture, with dangerous results.

Leaving the baby on a bed seems to be a mistake common among new parents. It's unwise to leave even a newborn in the middle of your big double bed without watching him. A little infant can push himself off faster than you imagine. And it's a long fall to the floor.

A six-month-old propped in a sitting position will often topple over after a few minutes, so be safe and keep him away from the edges of the bed.

Crawlers need protection, too. If your baby plays in his room, release the crib side and put it in the down position. There will be no possibility of the baby releasing the bar, allowing the side to strike him.

When your baby begins to stand, new problems arise. Remember to clear off all nightstands of pills that may have been left on them. Even aspirin can be a potential danger to a child.

Also check grandma's house for pills if your baby will be crawling around the bedrooms, unattended.

Kitchens

It's best to arrange your kitchen so that baby's high-chair or feeding table is away from the stove. Little fingers won't be able to touch the knobs, and spills won't hit your child.

And speaking of the stove; get into the habit of turning all pot handles inward so they can't be bumped accidentally.

Even plastic wrap, when handled by young children, is a hazard. The plastic sandwich bags that you use for left-overs should be stored in a drawer that's out of reach.

A dangling tablecloth can be enchanting to a toddler. If there's one on the table for dinner, beware of a small hand that may pull it off the table, dishes and all. Why not use placemats?

Until you can go to the hardware store for a lock, use elastic bands to bind together knobs of the cabinet under the sink where your cleaning supplies are stored. Enough of them will keep a child out, temporarily. If you're out of elastic bands, put a piece of sewing elastic through the handles and secure it with a large safety pin.

If your child still insists on getting into your cupboards, give him a special drawer that he may play in. Fill it with unbreakable containers, etc. and the other drawers should stay tidy. Good for grandma's house, too!

Glass plates break in every household. When this happens, wet some paper toweling or a handful of napkins. You'll be amazed at how the wet paper will catch those small pieces of glass that didn't come up with the broom.

It's best to put your garbage can inside a cabinet, rather than leaving it exposed to your toddler. Garbage is a source of fascination to a baby, but it can be dangerous.

If you don't have room behind a door for that garbage can, replace your old coverless one for the bright, new swinging-top type that children just can't get into.

When it's cleaning time, remember not to mix your cleaning "brews" with baby under foot. Spattering solutions can cause irritation to baby's skin or eyes.

If you must work in the kitchen and baby is roaming around on the floor, put a safety gate in the kitchen doorway. Baby can still watch you from the outside, but in safety.

Sockets

Electrical sockets are a source of danger often overlooked on a safety check. Is your child protected?

A quick treatment for those unused but exposed sockets is to cover them with adhesive tape or masking tape.

Your local hardware store has inexpensive plastic discs with prongs that fit into sockets. An adult can remove them, but they're immune to baby's fingers.

While you're in the store, inquire about the self-closing electric outlet that completely replaces the present socket unit. It takes longer to install but may be worth the effort in certain areas of the house.

And don't forget sockets in baby's room. They need covering, too, as well as those in the rooms where baby may wander.

One more cover-up: Just put the furniture in front of the sockets and the problem is solved. This is especially effective in baby's room where plugs are seldom used, but it's still better to use the plastic discs and be sure.

Windows

Even a toddler can push a screen out of position, so train your little ones not to lean against the open windows. There are some rules you should follow so that this problem won't arise.

Never place a chair directly in front of a window as a toddler can easily stand on it and in a minute push a loose screen out.

Never put a bed or crib underneath a window. The desire to stand on the window sill is very strong in curious toddlers.

Never leave a window open that has no screen in it. You're inviting trouble.

Doors

All glass doors should have safety glass. Even though it may cost more, it's worth the price. Save your pennies elsewhere!

Even a crawling baby can push a door open, so be prepared. From the time baby takes off on his own, keep all doors tightly shut. The outside world is too inviting to a small child.

If your front or back door doesn't always stay closed, it's time to install safety chains or hooks. Incidentally, when you put the safety chain on the door, put it high enough so that your older child cannot reach it by himself.

It's important to check all locks in the bedrooms and bathrooms to make sure your toddler can't lock himself in. Do you know how to release the locks from the outside of the rooms? You'd better learn!

It's easy to reverse the door locks in baby's room so that the danger of being locked in is eliminated. Once the lock is on the outside, your child is free from that frightening experience.

For other rooms where little feet shouldn't tread, those big door hooks work wonders if installed high enough on the outside of the door.

A great safety invention, the folding gate is a must for danger areas such as stairways. The gates come in two models. One must be screwed into the wall, making it stationary. The other type is a movable model that expands according to the width of the opening. If you have more than one area of danger, why not get the movable model and avoid having to buy a gate for each danger zone. And this kind is so easy to use.

Garages

Your safety check of the garage is an important one. Even though most children don't spend much time there, a few moments is long enough for trouble to begin.

Dad, construct some shelves at high level so that you can keep dangerous items out of bounds for small hands.

Do you have access to old kitchen wall cabinets? They make great garage storage units that can be locked easily with store-bought locks. Cabinets are even better than open shelves if little children are around.

66

Now that you have your storage areas, place your poisonous charcoal lighter way up high, even during the barbecue season. It's not a healthy drink on a hot day.

Remember to keep your matches in a safe place. Even a two-year-old can strike a match with a few practice sessions. Beware of stray matches indoors, too.

The garden tools: Mom's garden shears are too sharp for a tot to use. Trimmers could easily snip a finger instead of a weed. Any other tools belong on the shelf, too.

Garden sprays, bug sprays and other aerosol cans also belong off the garage floor. A spray sent in the wrong direction could be harmful to the child who gets caught in its path.

Little cowboys and Indians may be lured by the loose ropes and cords hanging in the garage. To prevent any tragedies, keep these props out of sight and reach.

Now, dad, put away your car supplies such as detergent, anti-freeze and polishes. Your son may decide to clean the car himself, when you're not around.

And speaking of cars, it's more convenient to leave the keys in the ignition but very dangerous for your child. It's best to train your young child to stay out of the car unless you're in it.

If you have an extra refrigerator in your garage, be sure to tie a rope around it or attach a lock, even if it means more work for you when you want to open the door.

If the refrigerator is not in use, turn it around so that the door is against a wall. Or you can remove the door, leaving no possibility of a child getting trapped inside.

Although it's easy to store empty soda bottles on the floor of the garage, it's not too smart. Children like to rearrange the bottles in the carton and could easily cut a finger by dropping one of these "toys." Isn't it easier to be safe and use a shelf?

Your electric garage door button isn't a toy, either. Why not make it a rule that only the older children and adults can do the pushing.

In A Hurry

When the door bell or phone rings and baby is crawling around the floor, do you protect him before answering the ring?

If you're ironing and this happens, don't forget to unplug the iron and put it in a safe place. Even if the call turns out to be a short one, the few seconds spent being cautious were worthwhile.

If you must leave the room suddenly, place baby in his playpen before you do. Then you won't have to worry if you're detained for a few minutes.

When an accident occurs and your car is gone for the day, immediately call the police; they'll have you on your way to the emergency room in no time. Don't waste time trying to locate friends or neighbors.

For those emergencies: Write the names and numbers of your doctors and the police and fire department on a small card and tape it to the bottom of your table phone. The numbers will always be ready for you or your sitter.

Street Safety

No child who steps outside of his house is too young to start learning the basic safety rules. And the teaching job belongs to the parents!

Holding hands with mommy or daddy is a good starting rule for toddlers. With short hops in and out of the car at shopping time, this is a must, even if you meet with strong resistence.

Even in lovely suburbia, trucks of all kinds are seen making their daily rounds. If you have a driveway, teach your run-abouts to expect those trucks to pull in and out without warning. Better yet, keep them off the driveway at playtime. Let it serve its real purpose, not be a playground.

Crossing streets without permission is bad practice for your younger child. Have him get accustomed to asking you to assist him or watch him cross in busy areas, at least until age four.

Children sometimes wander, so it's wise to teach your child two important but easy to remember facts. For self-identification, he should know his first and last name and the city in which you live. When he is around four, also teach him your phone number and street address. You may have to work on this for awhile, but it is worthwhile work.

He's now ready to face society, but one more reminder from you is necessary. The "talking to strangers" rule can present a dilemma to a parent, as too much warning can frighten a small child and not enough warning can be harmful.

It's best to tell your child not to talk to or take anything from unfamiliar people he may meet on the streets. Horrifying tales of what could happen are best avoided, especially with young children. This discussion requires some forethought before it's begun.

Off To School

Before kindergarten begins is the time to check these basic safety rules needed by school-age children.

A few trial walks to and from school are the most effective way of seeing if your safety discussions have been absorbed.

Ready to go? Walk on the sidewalks, not the streets. And cross only at the corners. Dashing across a street in the middle of the block is not to be recommended. When you reach the corners, have your child tell you when to cross. Make sure the "look left and right" rule is observed.

Most busy streets have safety guards in attendance, so teach your child how to obey the guard's signals. He's an important worker for your school district.

Has your son or daughter passed the test? If not, a few more walks around the neighborhood and to the school should bring results before the school bell rings.

More Safeguards

Dry cleaners supply us with more plastic bags than we need, so throw out any extras. But before you discard them, tie the bags in knots just in case the baby or toddler removes them from your wastebasket.

It's also wise to tie a knot in the bottom of any plastic coverings hanging in your closet. No chance of baby putting his head inside the open end.

Phone cords, especially the long-length cords, can entangle your child in seconds. Try a hook on the wall to hold the cord out of reach.

Other cords, such as lamp and appliance cords, can be shortened with a cord-shortening device sold in hardware stores that holds the excess cord.

Venetian blind cords are another source of danger. By cutting the loop made by the cord, you may prevent a small child from accidentally choking himself.

For the "just-beginning-to-stand" baby: Find some small squares of foam rubber and tape them to the four sharp corners of his favorite "grabbing" table. This will save many tears and scratches when baby clings to the table at practice time.

Make sure the older children don't leave any small articles around such as marbles, rings or ping-pong balls that a crawling baby could pick up and choke on.

Stairways, too, need to be checked for carelessly left toys. It's easy to trip on anything left on a stair, not just the roller skates.

The baby is really safest in the playpen, provided it's placed away from any hot radiators or portable window fans that could fall over. And never leave a child alone in a room with a portable space heater or fan.

traveling around

Once you leave home it becomes a trip, regardless of the distance you're going to be covering. A trip to the corner store with your child along is no longer as easy as it was when you could hop in the car by yourself or walk it alone. Many places even become too hard to step inside of with a newborn in your arms or an in-to-everything toddler at your side. But no one wants to stay home all of the time, so why not find the easiest ways to have fun with your tot, whether you are going to the store, a restaurant or on a vacation.

Ready, Set, Go!

The necessary ingredient for that well-organized, pleasurable visit is advance planning.

This is a must. An extra bottle and nipple should be left at grandma's or any home that you visit often. You won't have to rush home with your baby if you stop somewhere unexpectedly at feeding time, and you won't experience the frustration of hearing a newborn scream for his milk with no bottle in sight.

Keeping an extra pacifier at your parents' and in-laws' homes is a fine idea, too. It will save frantic moments searching for (or wishing for) the one you left home by mistake. And did you ever try to buy one on a Sunday night when all the stores are closed?

More advance planning: A portable crib, regardless of condition, makes an ever-ready place for baby to sleep at grandma's house. Just buy a used crib and paint it for a new look. Or rent one. Portable cribs can be leased for a nominal charge. This is a wise idea if you are staying out of town. Have your hostess rent one in advance from a local rent-all company.

Another wise idea for long stays at grandma's or a friend's is to make arrangements for diaper service to begin on your arrival date. Diaper service is available on a weekly basis as well as on a monthly plan.

And speaking of diapers, tuck a few disposables into your car's glove compartment so you can make unplanned visits to friends' houses without worrying about a wet baby. When you replenish the supply, you might think about a box for grandma's home.

Things to pack for traveling should include a supply of small plastic bags to put the soiled, wet diapers in. If you use paper bags, they'll tear and your nice diaper bag will look like a diaper pail, instead.

Also, bring along a large waterproof sheet or covering to put over the bedspread when it's time to change your baby. Your hostess will appreciate it and baby will be welcome for a second visit.

Save some of those TV dinner plates and pack them, too. They'll make meal time easier for both baby and you. When the meal is over just throw the plate away.

If you must take your young child to an adult gathering, tuck a pad of paper and a few crayons in your purse before leaving home. Let your young artist go to work when adult chatter begins to bore him, usually ten minutes after arrival time.

Car Safety

Perhaps the most difficult (and nerve-racking) part of traveling is the time actually spent en route and the worry over having to make sudden stops when your precious little ones aren't anchored securely to their seats. A few precautions are surely worth the effort.

An approved car seat should be a top priority item. And remember to use it, even for short trips. Make sure the car seat is appropriate for the age of the child.

If your infant is in a car bed, secure him with a strap or belt, so that he won't fly up in case of a sudden stop or collision. The car bed should be anchored.

See if you can put the baby's car seat on a seat that won't fold forward if you suddenly stop.

And investing in a second car seat, if you have two cars in which your child rides, is wise. You can probably buy the second one at a local thrift shop or house sale. There is no need to spend much money on this extra but do check to see if it is in good, safe condition.

If your little one is in a car seat close to the door, double-check the lock on that side. Babies and toddlers like to play with the various handles and could accidentally open the car door while you are driving. This is another reason to strap everyone in with safety belts.

The car safety experts would agree with that and also tell you that the safest place in the car for your child is on the seat directly behind the driver. Remember this next time your child insists on sitting up front with you.

Also make it a habit to check for little fingers before closing car doors. You can't depend on little children to watch out for their safety and to keep their hands away from the danger zones.

Nor can you count on them to keep their hands and arms where they should—inside. Try to set an example for your imitative toddler by keeping your own arm in the car. The excuse that "Mommy or Daddy does it" applies too often in this case.

Remember to lock all car doors when children are with you. See if your local hardware or car store has those safety gadgets that you put on the push-down car door locks. They're childproof and worth the price in your battle against those curious fingers.

No need to buy a ready-made first-aid kit. You can make your own and keep it in the glove compartment. It should consist of band-aids, tissue, first-aid cream or spray and any other necessities your family might need.

Traveling In Comfort

If you can leave your little ones at home when you're taking a lengthy car trip, you're lucky. If they are going along, good luck!

The best idea when you're taking a long motor trip and plan to sleep in different motels each night is to leave any child under three at home, if you can. By age three a child is usually trained, talking, eager and cooperative. In fact, a trip with a child three or over can be a joy for both you and him. You'll be amazed at how much even a three-year-old can absorb from a well planned trip.

73

Before leaving, why not take a short practice run in the car? You can show your child where he may or may not play, sit and sleep. Five minutes around the neighborhood should be enough.

When you're ready to leave, cover the back seat with an old blanket or sheet to keep cookie crumbs and other items from getting the upholstery dirty. Shake the debris off when you stop for food or gas and you're ready to go again in clean comfort.

For trained children, carry a package of disposable toilet seat covers. There will be no worry about sub-standard conditions often found en route. Any large department store should have the covers.

A car ride usually puts an over-tired and restless baby to sleep in the shortest time, so keep an extra crib blanket in the car to keep him warm during those unscheduled naps.

If you can work it, travel during your child's naptime and save your nerves. For a long return-trip home, start traveling around bedtime. If you are lucky, the children will sleep the whole time. This is perfect for that four or five hour drive.

Eating and Playing in the Car

For small children, a long car trip can be a time to play or a time to whine. You can really help them have a fun time with a bit of imagination and planning.

First, for your sake, insist that your kids leave their favorite talking or music-making toys and animals at home. Any tune, if repeated enough, will get on your nerves when you're in a car.

Playing cards are best left home, too, even though they're quiet. Nothing falls down the sides and under the seats more quickly than a deck of cards. Keep them hidden in a suitcase if you want them later for motel fun.

A surprise box makes traveling by car fun for all. Just fill a flat box with assorted toys and books and wrap each goodie in gay paper. When boredom sets in, let your child pick a present. Try to provide a new surprise for each day. If you keep the box under the front seat, it will be in easy reach.

Also take along a role of white shelving paper for your kids and they'll have hours of coloring fun on the trip. Rip off the amount desired at each drawing session, or let the artist keep coloring and re-rolling the paper.

74

Even your toddler can play simple car games such as, "I see a blue car, I see a red car." Try spotting certain models such as station wagons or convertibles. Traveling time will go by more quickly. You might even want to join in the fun.

Here's another easy game that should keep any child three and over settled for a few minutes. The winner is the first person to spot 10 red cars or 10 camping trailers, etc. Very simple and effective.

Now a time-saver. There's no need to waste 10 to 15 minutes of traveling time just for a soft drink. You can save time by bringing along packaged, powdered soft drink mixes and a thermos. When thirst hits, just stop at a gas station for some cold water and make your own instant refreshment in a jiffy.

Small juice cans from the baby food department are just the right size for travelers, young and old. Put a small straw in the can. When it's empty, just throw the can away.

Those little boxes of assorted cereals that come in the one serving size are easy to bring along, too, for a healthy snack-time treat. Each child can pick his favorite kind without any arguments.

You've Arrived

It's fun to go to someone's home for a change in routine, and even more fun to be invited back again as a family because you've been a smart, helpful guest.

If you put an old, thin blanket on the living room floor and put your pre-crawler on it, your baby will stay clean and so will the floor.

Borrow some large terry-cloth towels to put under the high chair when your baby is dining elegantly in a private home, especially if you're eating in a carpeted room. Cleaning up will be much easier, too.

And if you put a plastic placemat on top of the tablecloth at your child's place, the hostess will love you for it and you'll feel less frustration when the inevitable accident occurs.

One way to prevent those accidents is to make sure the child can easily reach his plate. It's so simple to convert any kitchen or dining room chair into a booster chair. Just pile some telephone books on top of the seat and let your darling eat away. Hint: A chair with arms will be safer.

Off To The Doctor

You'll be amazed at the number of trips you'll be making to the doctor for routine exams and those emergencies that hit every home. You might as well make the visits as easy as possible for both you and your child.

When going for those first few monthly check-ups, bring along a bottle filled with water or juice for your newborn. Babies often get fussy during the waiting room stay which can be a long and tiring one, even for mommy.

If you put a disposable diaper on your baby before going to the doctor's, you won't have to drag a wet diaper home with you. Don't forget to bring another for the change before the trip home, although most offices can supply you with one, if you forget.

Doctor's really don't care what the baby is wearing, as they usually see him after all the clothes have been removed. You might as well avoid buttons and frills when you visit the office and save yourself work.

It's easiest for all if you dress your baby in a one-piece outfit when you're going for that check-up. You can make a quicker exit with your screaming infant when the exam is over.

Tuck a pretzel stick or a few cookies in your purse to give your child after his physical, if he is crying non-stop. It might help to quiet him enough so you can dress him quickly and leave.

If the doctor wants to see your sick child in his office during the winter months, warm your car for a few minutes before placing the child in it. Start your car and then go back into the house and put your hats and coats on. The car will be warm when you're ready to leave.

Shopping Can Be Fun

Nothing lifts the spirits like a good shopping spree. If you're adorned with little ones you can still have fun, although it's not as easy as going solo.

For those shopping trips with your newborn along, why not place the infant seat on a reclining stroller seat and let him ride so that you won't have to carry the weight of your new, little package. That package can get very heavy after a few minutes!

No need to rush home from a shopping trip if baby's feeding time arrives earlier than you had planned. Most big department stores have lounges where you can feed baby a bottle or baby food in relative privacy. Expect some curious on-lookers, however.

Just be sure to carry plastic baby bottles, not glass, in your pocketbook. Glass breaks very easily and can make a mess of your bag if it's accidentally dropped.

Your hand-holding or baby-holding job will be easier if you carry a bag that has straps that hang or slip over your arms. This will free both of your hands for necessary jobs such as holding a toddler's hand when crossing the street or carrying him when he begs to be held. Leave the small-handled bags at home.

A big paper shopping bag will keep hats, mittens, jackets and sweaters together when your family goes on a shopping trip en masse.

It also will hold an extra pair of training pants when you're out with a child who is not completely trained. You'll save yourself the aggravation of having to run home if there is an accident.

Your key chain is a perfect place to hang some extra safety pins. You'll have an ever-ready emergency treatment for those buttons that pop off little dresses and coveralls.

If you end up pushing an empty stroller in a store as so often happens, while your little one walks, leave the stroller at home and put a baby harness around your active toddler. at least you'll be in control, and your child can't get too far away.

When you're caught with a hungry or cranky toddler in a department store, which often happens, rush to the food department and buy a slice of cheese or a big cookie. This will give you an extra ten or fifteen minutes in the store. It's bribery, but it works!

Graham crackers and miniature raisin boxes also help keep that climber in his stroller for a few extra minutes. Don't let your child see you putting these in your purse, however, or the treats may be eaten before you even reach the store.

A wet face cloth that you've put in a plastic bag is great for quick clean-ups after that messy treat. Dampened towel paper does the same job and can be left behind.

When you go food shopping, watch your climbing baby constantly if he's in a grocery cart. One fall is too many, so place him in the deep end of the cart until he is old enough to sit still. Then he can graduate to the front section. Again, bribery may work. Why not give your child some cookies or pretzel sticks to keep him still for a few more precious minutes?

Taking a Walk

For this kind of travel, strollers are a parent's delight!

If you can manage to get an extra stroller from some kind friend, take it, regardless of condition. Keep one in the car and one for those strolls around the neighborhood. No more lugging for you.

Hand-me-down strollers can look like new if you take a few minutes and paint the rusted chrome with silver paint. If the seat cover is in bad condition it can be replaced. Give your department store or local baby equipment company a call.

Umbrella strollers are so handy! Just make sure the baby's head and back are supported.

Hiker seats, or the extra seats, are available as an accessory for most regular strollers. If you have two children of stroller age, this attachment will be a good investment. Stroller graduates often like to stand with their feet on the back bar of the stroller and be pushed.

Little rattles and toys can be tied to the stroller with short strings so they won't get lost when they are dropped or thrown. Now your baby won't be able to play the "drop-it, pick-it-up" game with you.

If you tie a bright balloon to the front of his stroller, he'll have a gay time watching it as it moves...and hopefully he'll sit still for a little while.

If he's on a stroller strike, zip him into a baby harness for those walks. You can lengthen the reigns by adding an extra strap or piece of cord to the harness straps. Your toddler can have fun exploring and you'll know that he's always with you.

For the carriage-age baby: If the sun is shining directly into his eyes, just shift him to the foot of the carriage and he'll have a glare-free ride.

On icy winter days, spread baby oil on baby's cheeks to help prevent dryness and chapping of his delicate skin. Why not try some yourself while the bottle is still open?

Cycling

A great morale booster when you're weary from routine chores.

When you want to go cycling with your tiny infant, put him into an infant seat and then place the whole bundle into a large basket that's attached to the front handles of your bicycle. This will for work for the first few months.

For your child who is sitting up, the commercial child carrier that attaches to the back of an adult bicycle is perfect. For the restless child who doesn't always sit still, see if you can buy the type of seat that fits onto the front bar of the bike. This way you can keep a constant eye on him.

An adult's belt makes a perfect safety strap for a rear seat bicycle carrier. If your child tries to stand while you're pedaling, he's going to have some trouble.

Summer Fun

Summer never seems long enough. There are so many places to visit and see!

And there is no reason to leave your newborn at home. When you go to the beach, just bring along a large umbrella to set over his infant seat to prevent sunburn. Make sure it's secured well, however, and don't forget to guard baby from those curious sand-throwing toddlers who may wander over quietly.

Check with your pediatrician as to the safest way to give your baby a sun bath. A baby's skin is so delicate and must be protected from overexposure to that hot sun.

To avoid minor arguments over ownership of a shovel or pail, put an identifying symbol or a name on all the toys you take with you to a public beach or park.

Put an identifying symbol on your child, too! Let him wear a bright-colored swimsuit or beach hat to that crowded beach so you can quickly identify him.

If you are taking your pre-schoolers to a crowded beach, avoid taking a friend's child at all costs. You need to watch each child 100% of the time, a hard enough job with just your own.

For picnics and car trips, put condiments and small quantities of food into empty food jars. Throw the jars away when they are empties. The nice thing about this is there will be no dirty containers to carry home.

For easy drinks on a picnic, fill a plastic baby bottle with your child's favorite juice. When it's time to eat, take off the cap and insert a straw. Presto! A tall drinking glass for your older child.

And don't forget to take along some plastic bags filled with fruits and cookies for quick snacks when you're off to the beach or park.

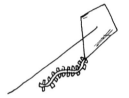

Eating in Restaurants

It's easier to just stay home for meals with children under three, but not as much fun as going out for dinner. Tiny tots don't care where they go so try to avoid the fancy spots when they're along. Unless you have a quiet, passive toddler, don't attempt to go to any restaurant where a quick exit is impossible. Your best place to dine is in a quick-service, drive-in type of restaurant. You'll avoid embarrassment if you must leave suddenly with your impatient child.

Bring along a TV dinner plate for easier dining with children under two. The waitress will be delighted to throw it away when the meal is over.

Packaged crackers help keep wee ones from getting restless while waiting for food in a restaurant. Have the waitress bring the crackers immediately. Paper and pencil to draw with help a hungry youngster wait quietly, too.

If possible, let your child sit in a seat facing a window so he can watch the cars and people go by. This is often enough diversion to keep a toddler or small child in his seat a little longer.

When you're caught without a bib in a restaurant make one yourself. Take a large napkin and knot one corner. Then tuck the knot into your child's top and spread the remaining sides out. It should resemble a butterfly, if you've made it correctly.

It's Time To Move

Moving day can be either a pleasure or a disaster. If you're about to relocate, the following hints may help divert a major tragedy.

If you're planning to move to a new city, just write the Chamber of Commerce in that city for information about your new home town. Share the findings with your children. Their doubts and anxieties may be lessened.

Let even your smallest child pick the color he wants for his bedroom in the new home. You'll give him a feeling of ownership and importance.

If grandma is willing and you're not moving far, let her keep your toddler during moving time. This will free you from the job of chasing him and protecting him from the movers and their loads.

And have your child's furniture put on the moving van last. It will be the first off the truck when it arrives and first inside your new home. Your youngster will feel at home in a very short time.

parties without panic

Party time officially arrives in the home when baby celebrates that all-important first birthday. From then on parties become a common occurence. The presence of a child in the house stimulates the party-giving mood, and there are birthdays and holidays to plan for year 'round. A certain degree of fussing is a necessary ingredient for a successful party, but if you handle it calmly, even your youngest should delight in the preparation. The secret to the successful affair, small or large, is the planning that takes place before that first guest arrives. The following hints should help make those happy times easier:

That First Birthday

This should really be a party in the parent's honor because they survived the difficult first year. Relatives are usually the only invited guests. Tell them to drop by for dessert after dinner or plan a pot-luck supper and have the party hour at dessert time. No need to disrupt baby's schedule, even on this important day.

Don't forget to have the camera loaded for gift-opening time as well as for the candle-blowing ceremony. Place baby in the high chair so he can't accidentally tumble onto the lighted cake. Keep little fingers from the candles, too!

Have a pretty bib ready for eating time so your one-year-old won't ruin his outfit. He's still too young to be expected to be neat.

The Terrible Twos

Birthday number two follows so quickly it's hard to believe. By now your child has probably acquired some little friends, making it a fun time to invite the toddlers over for cake and ice-cream.

If you are really ambitious, try planning a simple early hour luncheon with birthday cake as dessert. Then all the tired twos can go home for naps on schedule.

An hour is long enough for the little ones when more than four guests are present. You'll find it long enough, too!

3:30 or 4:00 p.m. is another favorite time for the young set. The one drawback is that the party goodies fill their tummies and dinner food is ignored. But if you're not a nutrition nut, it doesn't really matter.

When you're doing the inviting, why not ask each guest to bring a high chair or youth chair along? The guests will be more comfortable and there will be less chance of accidents. If you live in a third-story walk-up, better make other arrangements.

If you're short on table space, put your paper or vinyl cloth on the kitchen floor and create a make-shift table for the toddlers. No chairs to worry about, and what a delight at clean-up time.

Hide your valuables with great care before the door-bell rings. Most children won't be as well-trained as yours.

Fido should be out of sight, too. He belongs on a leash, outside if possible, to keep him away from the gifts, guests and other goodies. He'll be happier, too, away from all the confusion.

Enlisting a friend to serve as photographer is wise. That way you won't miss out on the best shots. While you bring out the cake, she can do the snapping.

The Nursery School Set

When your child reaches three or four the tone of the birthday parties changes. If your child attends nursery school, his peer group has increased and friends are school chums as well as the children of your friends and neighbors.

This may be the occasion to increase the youthful guest list and decrease the number of adults present. This age group seems content to stay alone at a friend's for an hour or so. Plan accordingly.

And if the adults aren't present, think of all the pre-cleaning and coffee that can be eliminated. Only a group of 10 or so children to contend with, who won't notice a little dust.

Bring out assorted toys and crayons before the children arrive so they can get busy right away before they become bored waiting for the late-comers.

It's best to invite children of the same age level. Game planning is so much easier when you don't have to worry about pleasing the "too-young" child.

On the invitations that go out around a week or so before the party, write "regrets only" instead of RSVP. You'll get fewer calls that way. You'll always have one or two who won't respond and who may even forget the day. It happens. Take it in stride.

When gift-giving time arrives, have a container nearby the wrappings. And remove the new games to a safe spot before the young guests open them out of curiosity and misplace pieces.

If a younger sibling is around at gift-giving time, hand him a new, inexpensive toy in gift wrapping to avoid hurt feelings. He's too young to understand that soon he, too, will have parties of his own.

Favors and Other Goodies

A birthday party is not a party to a child unless the room is decorated at least a little.

Party plates, napkins and cups are so abundant now that you can choose from an endless variety of styles, colors and prices. Why not use your own gay vinyl cloth and work from there? Get color-coordinated plates and napkins. These can be obtained in the paper goods section of the grocery store as well as in the more expensive "party" section. Suit your taste and budget.

It's fun to have balloon place markers tied to the backs of the chairs. Blow up the balloons, take out the magic marker, and write the appropriate name on each.

Balloons are a favorite favor, regardless of age, so have plenty around from the start of the party 'til go-home time. And have extras for those that pop at the last minute. Tears can spoil the party mood.

Home-made favors can be made if you do some pre-party planning. Take the supply of bathroom tissue tubes you've saved, fill them with candy and cover them with wrapping paper or crepe paper. Tie the ends with string or ribbon.

Identical favors for the girls and for the boys will keep the comparison of goodies to a minimum and eliminate jealousy and tears.

It's best to have a "surprise" bag ready for departure time. Any brown bag, such as a lunch sack, will do. Put each child's name on the bag with a gay marker, add a touch or two of decoration, and they'll look quite appealing.

If you want to splurge a bit more, use the commercial party bags sold at most discount stores. Fill them with favors and candy, and the children will leave happily.

When you're really stumped as to what to buy as favors, remember that you can always divide items such as four-pack clay sets and soap sets into single units.

Plan to have everyone ready at least five minutes before the official departure time. Much confusion will be avoided when the parents start arriving to take the tired guests home.

If a younger child comes along, he'll be thrilled if you give him a balloon or some candy that you've saved just for this purpose. He would have had a hard time getting some from his sister or brother on the way home!

If you need a centerpiece for the birthday table, bring out the pretty cake. What could be more enticing to a young child's appetite?

For the three and unders, it might be smart to let each child have a cupcake, or **miniature birthday cake, instead of a slice of a big cake. They'll all feel important and very special.**

To save mess for both you and your young guests, make a sponge cake or angel food cake instead of the traditional frosting-laden birthday cake. They won't know the difference and might even like this type of cake better. Decorate it with some gum drops. What a sight!

If you are ambitious and decide to make your own cake, there's no reason to have it look un-partyish. With all the cake decorating tubes and kits available, everyone can be a successful baker.

Miniature colored marshmallows make gay cake decorations. Ice-cream sprinkles also will give color and appeal to an otherwise plain cake.

Forget to buy candle holders? Then use some gum drops. They work fine as do the left-over miniature marshmallows.

An easy way to serve the ice-cream is to make balls and freeze them in cup-cake papers a day before the party. Put them in a cupcake pan so they won't stick together.

Theme Birthday Parties

Parties can take many different forms, depending on your desires and imagination. A birthday party can be traditional, like the ones you had as a child, or follow a theme for variety. A theme chosen according to the month, such as an April Showers party, will make decoration planning easier and will add interest for the party-goers.

If the party is for the younger set, thrill them with a live clown. No need to hire a professional (although they are available for kid's parties). With a borrowed wig, some make-up and funny clothes, dad can do a superb job. He'll enjoy it, too, despite what he may say!

A costume party always makes the occasion livelier. Have the kids come in their Halloween costumes. Prizes can be awarded, if you consider yourself a good "judge."

Tea parties for the girls and cowboys and Indians parties for the boys are sure successes. No need to segregate the sexes, however. Mixed parties are just as easy, especially for the parents of sons, because girls tend to quiet things down.

Lucky the parents with a summer-born child. The outdoors lends itself to innumerable possibilities. Pray for sunshine, but have an alternative plan handy.

If you've scored with the weather, put a sign on the front door telling guests to come around to the backyard. Not a speck of dirt should enter your home.

Picnic parties are always a hit. You can have lunch already packed in sacks or do just the "dessert" party. Both will be enjoyed if a festive mood prevails.

In case you don't have a backyard that's suitable, tell the moms to meet you at a local park or playground, or you be the chauffeur. Set a specific time and enjoy an hour or so in the sunshine while the kids romp around. Don't forget the cake, juice and favors, however.

Children born in winter can also have a picnic-type party. Make sack lunches, but let them eat indoors on blankets. Kids are flexible.

With any party, it's best to make a schedule of activities and games ahead of time. Time can go slowly when you're in charge of 10 or more eager children. Plan a few extra activities so there's no time for restlessness or uncontrolled horseplay.

Games

Games seem to be handed down from generation to generation. Relay races, treasure hunts, hot potato game, clothespin-in-the-bottle, and others are still popular. Ask your child about his favorites.

Pin-the-Tail-on-the-Donkey has survived the generation gap. You can still buy it as a ready-made game, but if you prefer make your own adaptation. Take a sheet, draw a clown face on it, supply paper noses and pins. The rules are the same. Or if it's Halloween season, try pinning the stem on the pumpkin.

Using scotch tape instead of pins when playing this game will save wear and tear on your walls and protect little fingers.

Don't forget to put the child's name on his tail. A little one won't always remember the number assigned to him.

Hunting for candy is another favorite with the young set. Hide a big bag of candy, preferably outdoors, and let the children search around. Always keep a little extra in case one child is a slowpoke and returns empty-handed. Small, wrapped candies work best.

A lollypop hunt at the end of a party gives a happy send-off. Scatter a bag or two of pops all over the yard and let the children loose. Kids love this. Again, make sure you've saved a handful of extras so that everyone gets something.

Reading a story as a closing activity will calm the younger ones down before they go home. It's especially effective with the five-and-under crowd as pick-up time nears.

Other Occasions

Birthdays needn't be the only time you plan a special day for your child. The calendar is filled with joyous occasions when you can put your talents to use.

Supper time can be turned into a "family" party on such days as Valentine's Day, Halloween and other fun dates. An appropriately decorated cake and special napkins are all that are needed to make a regular day special.

Halloween is always a child's delight. Be sure to discuss safety rules before sending the kids out trick-or-treating. And don't forget to enlarge the holes in store-bought masks. Better yet, forget the masks and use make-up instead.

The summer sandpail makes a great container for all the Halloween goodies, especially for your pre-schooler. Send the kids out early enough to avoid the crowds.

What Helpful Hints Do You Have?

The hundreds upon hundreds of suggestions in this book are not just my own ideas. They come out of the practical experience of many, many friends, relatives, neighbors, and acquaintances.

Perhaps you have a child-care tip that has worked for you, that you feel I should include in a subsequent edition of this book, or in some other work. I'd be delighted to receive your suggestion, with the understanding that I have your unqualified permission to publish it. Please send your hint to:

Nanci R. Weinfeld
1712 S. Highland
Arlington Heights, Ill. 60005

Thanks!
Nanci

Notes

Notes